Out Loud

THE BEST OF RAINBOW RADIO

Edited By Ed Madden and Candace Chellew-Hodge

Hub City Press
Spartanburg, SC

First printing, August 2010

Hub City editor: Betsy Wakefield Teter
Cover design: Robin Ridgell
Interior book design: Corinne Manning
Proofreaders: Carol Bradof, Candace
Lamb, Jameelah Lang, Jan Scalisi
Printed by McNaughton & Gunn in
Saline, MI

Library of Congress
Cataloging-in-Publication Data

Out loud: the best of Rainbow
radio / edited by Ed Madden and
Candace Chellew-Hodge.
p. cm.
Edited transcripts from the radio
show, Rainbow radio.
ISBN 978-1-891885-76-1
1. Gay culture—South Carolina.
2. Gay culture—Southern States.
3. Rainbow radio (Radio program)
   E. Madden, Ed, 1963-
II. Chellew-Hodge, Candace, 1965–
III. Rainbow radio (Radio program)
HQ76.96.O87 2010
306.76'609757—dc22
2010006749

Out Loud is funded in large part by the Freeman Foundation of San Francisco, CA.

Hub City Press
186 W. Main St.
Spartanburg SC 29306
864.577.9349
www.hubcity.org

For Harriet Hancock

table of contents

listening

learning

resisting

contributors

Acknowledgements

THANK YOU TO THE STAFF OF RAINBOW RADIO: the show's co-hosts, Bruce Converse and Candace Chellew-Hodge; our occasional substitute hosts, Larry Hembree and Pat Patterson; show producers Jim Blanton, Bert Easter, Harriet Hancock, and Ed Madden; and sound engineers Larry Farina, Jordan Jennings (at WUSC, for the student voices), and Candace Chellew-Hodge; as well as to our many wonderful guests over the first three years. Thanks also to the board and volunteers of the South Carolina Gay and Lesbian Pride Movement (now South Carolina Pride) and the Harriet Hancock Community Center, the community sponsors of Rainbow Radio. We would also like to thank Robin Ridgell for our fabulous logo, Keith Blanton (aka Kiki Merlot) and others who organized community fundraisers for the show, and the South Carolina Gay and Lesbian Business Guild, a critical source of community allies and sponsors.

We are also thankful to the Freeman Foundation and the Ketner Fund, which offered us matching grants in our first years—grants that not only supported the show but also helped us to build our listener base. We are deeply grateful to the Fund for Southern Communities in Atlanta, which honored the show with a Media Justice grant, and the

Human Rights Campaign of the Carolinas, which recognized the show's groundbreaking work with the Equality Award in 2007.

Thanks also to Betsy Teter and the board and staff of the Hub City Writers Project, and to our indefatigable editorial assistant, Darien Cavanaugh. Also special thanks to *Q-Notes* in Charlotte and the *Free Times* in Columbia, in which some of these essays first appeared in print.

Finally, we must thank Trey Greene at WOIC 1230 AM and Inner City Radio, who first contacted us to suggest that there should be a gay and lesbian radio talk show on Columbia's Air America affiliate. If he hadn't made that first contact, we never would have found ourselves out loud on the airwaves of South Carolina.

Rainbow Radio: An Introduction

I.

IN AUGUST OF 2005, an ad began to air on South Carolina's Air America station, WOIC 1230 AM in Columbia. "For far too long," the announcer stated, "talk radio airwaves have been dominated by the people who talk about us. Starting this fall, we speak for ourselves! Tune in on Sundays at 10 a.m., beginning October 9, for Rainbow Radio: The Real Gay Agenda. Listen to the voices of gay and lesbian South Carolinians as we tell our own stories about who we are, what we do, and how we are going to change this state." The first show aired on October 9, set to coincide with the annual celebration of National Coming Out Day on October 11.

What began as an experiment—South Carolina's first ever gay and lesbian radio show—has grown into a real grassroots-driven radio program with broad community involvement. And what began with a six-week commitment has turned into over four years of unprecedented local radio programming, offering diverse, accurate, and often unparalleled representations of South Carolina's gay and lesbian communities.

Rainbow Radio offered stories most of us have never heard in South Carolina media before.

In 2005, about the time a group of volunteers from the South Carolina Gay and Lesbian Pride Movement first met with folks from WOIC to talk about the show, Garrison Keillor (of *A Prairie Home Companion*) wrote about the joys of listening to radio in *The Nation*: "You twiddle the dial," he wrote, "and in the midst of the clamor and blare and rackety commercials you find a human being speaking to you in a way that intrigues you and lifts your spirits." For us, that's Rainbow Radio, a place where, as Keillor might say, you can hear "a fellow American telling a story unlike all the other stories. Pretty amazing. And all the more so for showing up on a dial full of blathering idiots and jackhammer music."

Pretty amazing.

On Rainbow Radio, those stories have included one woman's brave and devastating story about the drowning of her partner and horrific treatment by her partner's family, a Citadel cadet's moving account of his struggles with depression, and Becci Robbin's heartbreaking tale of a dying man's last visit to church. They have also included David Gillespie's and Candace Chellew-Hodge's affirming accounts of being gay and Christian, lesbian activist Melissa Moore's praise of strong Southern women, and Richland County Sheriff Leon Lott's comments on equal treatment. We've heard from a Spartanburg school teacher, an African-American slam poet, and the state's first lesbian Congressional candidate. We have had Stacy Smallwood's thrilling take on the black gay experience, Wilhelmina Hein's personal journals of her transgender transition, memoirist Sheila Morris's tales of growing up lesbian in rural Texas, and fourteen-year-old Tommy Gordon talking about his gay uncle.

Guests on Rainbow Radio have included celebrities like comedian Lily Tomlin (just before her performance at Columbia's Koger Center) and actor Leslie Jordan (before his appearance at the Human Rights Campaign dinner in Charlotte), and programs have featured telephone interviews with activists, authors, and experts from across the nation. But the focus of the show, especially those first couple of years, was on the people, the stories, and the issues of gays and lesbians in

South Carolina and the South. Every episode ended with a commentary, an essay, or a story. I had the extraordinary pleasure of soliciting, editing, and collecting those stories. I was repeatedly struck by the power and singularity of these voices—these are, after all, gay and lesbian voices from the Deep South—but also struck by their authenticity. These are people speaking from the particularities of experience in a culture that denies them legitimacy, even as it grounds them and gives them strength.

We've broadcast empowering interviews about being out in Greenville, Rock Hill, Myrtle Beach, and Aiken. In 2005 and 2006, Rainbow Radio also included several shows on South Carolina's gay and lesbian families. The 2000 U.S. Census told us that South Carolina ranks fourth in the nation for same-gender couples raising children at home, and that there are gay and lesbian couples in every county in this state. We wanted South Carolina to know that our families are part of the fabric of this state. Rainbow Radio gave voice to a community that is all too often ignored, demonized, and demoralized by the messages they hear from their politicians, their preachers, and sometimes their own families.

When that group of community activists—Bruce Converse, Bert Easter, Kate Goodrich, Harriet Hancock, Ed Madden, and Alvin McEwen (and soon thereafter Jim Blanton and Candace Chellew-Hodge)—began work on the show in the summer of 2005, the original goal was, as our first promotional ad suggested, to get our voices into mainstream media and to tell the truth about our lives and our families. But the introduction of a constitutional amendment banning same-sex marriage in the South Carolina legislature in 2005 gave this work added urgency. In November 2006, South Carolina passed a constitutional amendment that denied any legal recognition—not just marriage, but civil unions, partner benefits, or any form of family recognition—to unmarried couples and their children. Faced with legislation that said some families deserve protection and other families—our families— don't, we felt that telling our stories mattered more than ever. Several of the essays collected here refer to that amendment campaign and its effects on our families.

In this book, we have tried to suggest the range of voices on the show, as well as the poignancy and power of those stories—and the cultural, political, and educational work of Rainbow Radio. Selection was difficult, and sadly we were unable to include some important voices—not just because there were so many, but because the social pressures that silence gay and lesbian voices continue to constrain our own contributors. One woman—the one who wrote so movingly about her partner's death—feared for her job security and faced increasing family hostility after her story first aired; not only were we unable to include her voice in Out Loud, but she also asked us to delete her commentary from our online archives.

Originally we had thought to group them by topic—Family, Identities, Culture, Community, Activism—but such divisions belie the many echoes and broader themes that connect these works, so we put them in three clusters: Listening, Learning, Resisting. Listening addresses what we listen to, what we listen for, and how we listen (or don't listen) to one another. Learning is about how we learn who and what we are, the cultural and societal messages that too often stigmatize and silence (or sometimes quietly empower and sustain). The voices of Resisting suggest the many ways we learn to live with and resist those messages, both in our individual lives and through community activism.

Throughout the book people define themselves—not only as gay, lesbian, queer, transsexual, family members, allies, but also by religion and region. Most are Southern, though a few find themselves here in the Deep South for school or work. Some writers use the GLBT or LGBT (sometimes LGBTQ) as a blanket acronym for gay, lesbian, bisexual, transgender, and queer communities.

Although the show's on-air footprint was small, limited mostly to Columbia, our listening audience was wide—with podcasts on the web reaching listeners as far away as Wisconsin and Australia, as well as grateful listeners who contacted us from the rural areas of this state—Aynor, Greer, Lake City, Greenwood, Summerville, Florence, Orangeburg. In 2007, the Human Rights Campaign of the Carolinas presented Rainbow Radio the 2007 Equality Award, recognizing the program's educational outreach and political impact, and in 2008 the Fund for Southern Communities, an Atlanta-based social justice fund, awarded

Rainbow Radio a "media justice" grant in recognition of the importance of this grassroots media work. I am so proud to have been a part of this work.

—Ed Madden

II.

RAINBOW RADIO has been the longest six weeks of my life.

Six weeks, that's all Ed Madden asked for when he called to tell me that WOIC had granted them a half-hour for the first radio show designed specifically by gay and straight people, for gay and straight people. Six weeks turned to twelve, twelve to twenty-four, and on and on it went until, at this writing, Rainbow Radio has been on the air for more than four years.

Ed didn't have to do a lot of selling to me, or to my co-host, Bruce Converse. Both of us are old radio dogs. I got my start at the age of seventeen, as a DJ for an AM/FM combo that broadcast out of a trailer park in Buford, Georgia. I stayed in media for some twenty years, eventually moving out of radio and into broadcast news writing.

Bruce and I both remember the good old days of radio—doing the "rip-and-read" (grabbing wire copy from the AP or UPI wire machine and reading it "cold," or without rehearsal), recording on reel-to-reel machines, splicing tape on the reel-to-reel (which is a lost art thanks to newfangled computer audio programs), and using "carts"—big plastic eight-track-esque cartridges that had enough tape in them to loop a thirty-second or sixty-second commercial. (Am I so old that I need to define "eight-track" as well? If you must know, try Wikipedia.)

So, when the offer to do a radio show after being off the air since the mid-1990s came, I jumped at it, as did Bruce. The first recording session took about three hours as we all crammed into a tiny, and increasingly warm, studio at WOIC (they have since upgraded us to a larger studio, which now contains only Bruce and me—go figure), got to know one another, and plotted out the show. Bruce, God bless him, brought a script along. He's done that for every subsequent show as well, becoming the show's main writer.

The format of the show shook out fairly quickly—an introduction of news and banter between Bruce and me, then into an interview with a guest or two, sometimes three or more, then a commentary and a closing. Each week's recording had a party atmosphere as producers Ed and Jim "jb" Blanton, engineer Larry Farina, and Bruce and I would crowd into the studio. Each blooper, each slip of the tongue, and each joke would often send us in to fits of laughter that would delay taping a good ten to fifteen minutes.

"Y'all are my therapy every week," Larry would tell us—every week. We were also therapy for one another, a bright spot in the week, getting together to laugh, cut-up, cry, and generally make history in South Carolina.

As I read through the essays presented in Out Loud, my heart swells with pride. I am proud of the show—its producers, hosts, engineers, and every volunteer who has put heart and soul into making it a quality half-hour filled with news, humor, drama, enlightenment, and tear-jerking stories. The voices on Rainbow Radio have been muted for so long, silenced not just by society's homophobia but the internalized homophobia of our own community. Rainbow Radio has given voice to the silent, and now, through these pages, those voices are further amplified.

What a long, strange, and wonderful six weeks it's been.

—Candace Chellew-Hodge

Tommy Gordon

My Uncle Greg is Gay

MY UNCLE GREG IS GAY. This has never been an issue because I have grown up knowing he is gay. My grandmother, Harriet Hancock, bought me a book called *Uncle What-Is-It Is Coming*. The book is about two kids who have a gay uncle who is coming to their house to visit. The children don't know what "gay" means, so they go around the neighborhood asking others what it means. The kids get very stereotypical answers—you know, like Carmen Miranda and leather guys. But when their uncle arrives, they see that he is just like everyone else. He plays games with them, and he is a really fun guy. They learn that he doesn't like brussels sprouts either.

That is what I want people to know about my uncle: that he is a really neat guy, who has a really neat dog, and we have lots of fun when he comes to visit us from Atlanta. Once we all went to the beach together when I was about five years old—my mom, step-dad, grandmother, aunt and uncle, and three cousins. I remember that Uncle Greg was on the deck and he was reading a book by David Sedaris called *Naked*. I ran into the house and told my Aunt Karen that Uncle Greg was on the deck and he was reading *Naked*. She told me to tell him to "go put some clothes on." They all thought that was so funny.

When I was five years old I went to a gay pride march in Myrtle Beach. I was proud to stand on the stage next to my uncle and recite the Pledge of Allegiance. There was a lot of opposition to that march. One of the largest developers in Myrtle Beach did everything they could to stop the march. My grandmother got so upset when the mayor of Myrtle Beach called gay people "garbage." That kind of talk from a person who is in a position of power proves that these marches are necessary for education and understanding.

At recent marches there have been street preachers and protesters lined up on the sides of the streets of Columbia. There is one protester that everyone jokes about being my grandmother's own personal protester, because he showed up at two functions where my grandmother was being honored for her work with the gay and lesbian community. I walked over to him and told him that "Jesus never taught me to hate."

Something that I really dislike about some people is that they are so judgmental. Sometimes they are so judgmental and so filled with hate that they want to beat up gay people. One of my friends that I met at a gay pride festival was beaten up because he is gay. And I know that a young man named Matthew Shepard was brutally beaten to death because he was gay. It really bothers me when I hear people talking bad about gay people when they don't even know a gay person—especially politicians—because ignorant people will listen to their hate and their bigotry.

I've been to many South Carolina legislative sub-committee meetings with my grandmother. It seems like politicians here are always trying to pass laws against gay people, like the right to marry and the right to adopt children. My mom tells me the story about my first legislative sub-committee hearing. She took me there when I was only four months old. The South Carolina House of Representatives was considering a bill to prevent gays and lesbians from adopting children. My Uncle Greg was there holding me, standing beside my grandmother as she tried to explain that if anything happened to my parents, Uncle Greg would be the best person to adopt me, and if they passed that law he wouldn't be able to.

I think things will change for gay people because they are tired of being in the closet and they are talking about their rights. I hope that by the time I'm grown that things will be different, and people will have learned to accept people for who they are.

Tommy Gordon was fourteen years old when he read this essay on Rainbow Radio in fall of 2005.

Ed Madden

A Soundtrack for Coming Out

NATIONAL COMING OUT DAY is celebrated every year on October 11. Rainbow Radio went on the air on October 9, 2005. Celebrating both National Coming Out Day and the debut of the show, the first show concluded with this commentary by Ed Madden. A version of the essay also aired on the first anniversary show in 2006.

It was 1984, maybe 1985. I was hanging out in the college newspaper office, proofreading, gulping coffee, gossiping. And then someone put in a cassette tape. Even now, as I recall that moment, the words to the song still stun me: "Contempt in your eyes as I turn to kiss his lips." His lips. This was a song sung by a man, about kissing another man.

The album was *Age of Consent* by the Bronski Beat. The song was "Why?" Years later I would discover that the song was an anthem of gay liberation in Britain at the time, with the chorus, "You and me together, fighting for our love." But I didn't know that then. All I knew was the shiver of recognition, fear, and power—*power* really seems the best word—that I felt hearing that song for the first time.

Tuesday is National Coming Out Day, which is celebrated every October 11 to commemorate the 1987 march on Washington, DC, for gay and lesbian rights. The day also draws attention to the need for gay and lesbian people to come out—to their families, their neighbors and co-workers, their elected officials.

Coming out as a gay or lesbian person not only changes your own life, it changes the culture around you. Studies have shown that people who know someone gay or lesbian are more likely to oppose discrimination and to support the rights of gays and lesbians.

During the debates over marriage equality in the South Carolina legislature, a religious group sent legislators a pamphlet filled with myths and stereotypes about gay people. It was laughable stuff, if you know gay and lesbian people, but many legislators don't. And if we are not out as gay and lesbian people, defining ourselves, challenging the myths, then other people will define us.

I didn't know any gay or lesbian people when I was growing up in rural Arkansas, and I had little information about homosexuality. When I heard Bronski Beat singing about a gay kiss, I was sitting on the campus of a small fundamentalist college in rural Arkansas. I was vice president of my fraternity, beau for a sorority, and president of the College Republicans. In that hotbed of male privilege, heterosexuality, and conservative politics, I was struggling with my own sexual identity.

It would be several more years before I would have the courage to come out, to be honest with myself and my family. But those songs offered a message that was for me, at that moment, transformative.

Coming out takes courage. As Michael Haigler, former president of the South Carolina Gay and Lesbian Business Guild, says, "It doesn't take courage to blend." But when you live in a hostile culture, courage can be hard to find.

For many gay and lesbian people, popular culture can offer a lifeline of affirmation. Politicians may deny the rights—even the existence—of their gay and lesbian constituents. The South Carolina legislature may pass laws prohibiting marriage and civil unions. Republican Senator Jim DeMint may state that he thinks gay schoolteachers should be fired. The Horry County School Board might remove gay-positive books from the school libraries, as they did only a few years ago. Your school, your community, your legislature, your church, even your family may offer only negative messages, but the voices of popular culture still get through.

Whether it's Will and Grace or Rosie and Ellen on television, or Melissa Etheridge and Rufus Wainwright on the radio—or Rainbow Radio on Air America!—the message gets through: the message that you are not alone, that you are not evil, that your life is valuable, that there are communities of support out there for you.

On Tuesday, I'm going to be playing Bronski Beat and the Pet Shop Boys and Pansy Division, the music that let me imagine a different culture and a different version of myself—my own personal soundtrack for coming out. If you happen to stop by, please forgive me if you hear me trying to sing along. "You and me together, fighting for our love."

Candace Chellew-Hodge

Do You Like Cris Williamson?

"DO YOU LIKE CRIS WILLIAMSON?"

A seemingly simple question, but in reality a loaded question—a question whose answer was not one to be taken at face value, but a question that sought a deeper, encoded answer.

"Do you like Cris Williamson?"

The question was always asked by one woman to another—not merely for informational purposes or idle chit chat, but to elicit a knowing response.

Depending on the answer, you knew whether the woman being asked the question was part of the family, played for your team—well, you get the picture.

"Do you like Cris Williamson?"

If the woman looked at you with a puzzled look and said, "Who's Cris Williamson?" then you knew she most likely belonged to the other family or played for the other team. Time to quickly move on to other questions and find a way to excuse yourself from the conversation sooner rather than later. If she smiled knowingly and said, "Oh, yes," then you knew you were at a family reunion, or at least in the same ballpark.

"Do you like Cris Williamson?"

It was an early-to-mid-1980s form of gaydar for me. If a woman looked to me like family, or a member of my team, I'd chat her up and ask her, "Do you like Cris Williamson?" because only lesbians—um, I mean family members and team players—would know about the lesbian singer who came to prominence in the mid-1970s.

Her seminal 1975 album—if any work by a lesbian can be called "seminal"—*The Changer and the Changed*, was a collection of wonderful songs that would make any member of the Island of Lesbos happy. Her alto voice singing about waterfalls and the ache of lost love transported me as a young dyke. It made me feel less alone in the world, less ashamed to be a member of this particular family, a rookie on this particular team. We often sang her "Song of the Soul" at a Metropolitan Community Church in Atlanta I attended—all of us singing: "Follow your heart, love will find you/Truth will unbind you/Sing out a song of the soul."

Cris had followed her heart, love had found her, truth had unbound her, and she sang shamelessly about a Sweet Woman: "A little passage of time 'til I hold you and you'll be mine/ Sweet woman, risin' so fine." And she wasn't singing about her friend who happened to be a girl. No, this was a woman who was not afraid to sing about loving women and being loved by women. If another woman liked Cris Williamson, you could be sure that wasn't the only woman she liked—*that* way.

"Do you like Cris Williamson?" It's a question that served me well in a time when Melissa Etheridge was still in the closet and the Indigo Girls were first emerging and weren't yet brave enough to sing about being queer. But when you saw them, you just knew that if you could ask Melissa, Amy, and Emily, "Do you like Cris Williamson?" you'd most likely get an emphatic, "Yes."

You just knew they were family. You just knew they played for your team, but even they were flying under the gaydar back then. They all had to be careful, or they'd end up like Cris Williamson. She never made it to the big time like Melissa and the Indigo Girls because she so openly declared her family affiliation, her team status, with every album she produced. But, she built a long-lasting career by boldly going where other family members and team players dared not go. She garnered success where it mattered—among her family, among her teammates—and there she was famous, so famous she could become a codeword, a precursor to gaydar that was nearly foolproof.

Questions like, "Do you like Melissa Etheridge?" or "Do you like the Indigo Girls?" don't work because they are famous enough to have straight followings. It's only the likes of Cris Williamson, Holly Near, and Meg Christian who can tease out even the most reticent dyke among us.

So, the next time your gaydar gets jammed, don't be afraid to go with the classic that always works. Look them in the eye, smile sweetly and ask:

"Do you like Cris Williamson?"

Bruce Converse

Opening Up

Father's Day 2006

IT WAS SPRINGTIME, 1985, and it was time to open up the summer house.

My family has owned a summer house in the woods of northern Wisconsin since the mid-1940s. When I had moved back to Chicago in 1980 after a few years away, I picked up the family ritual of opening up the summer house every spring.

Built between 1936 and 1938, the house in Minocqua has three bedrooms, two baths (one with a claw-footed tub), a kitchen, and a large combined dining and living room. This room and one of the bedrooms each has a natural stone fireplace. Along the left side of this large combination room are windows opening onto a large screen porch. This porch overlooks a natural, spring-fed lake. The house has no central heat, so it can only be used about four or five months out of the year. My first visit to this great old house was when I was three. I had made it up there almost every year after that.

The plumber would have already turned on the water and the cleaning lady would have cleaned the bathrooms and vacuumed the floors. Most of the furniture from that large porch off the living room would have been stored in the front bedroom, just off the kitchen, to protect it from the winter elements. Part of the opening-up consisted of moving the furniture back out onto the large front porch.

During the winter months, curtains were put over the eighteen windows in the house in order to keep out the bleaching sunlight, reflecting off the mountains of snow that would fall, as well as to keep prying eyes from looking in. These covers had to be removed and put away.

Unless the cleaning lady had done so, all five beds had to be made. Putting away the sheets that had covered all the furniture, filling the wood boxes, sweeping off the porch steps, putting out clotheslines and bird feeders were also opening-up chores.

That particular year, 1985, Dad decided to go north with me for this annual opening-up ritual, which was scheduled over a long weekend. I had told my folks earlier that year that "my roommate" and I were going to part company. Maybe he sensed that I needed something, maybe he knew Stephen had been more than a "roommate."

It was a difficult time for me. I had been with Stephen for five years when we had a sudden breakup right before my birthday in February. Stephen was from Wisconsin, and had finally moved back to Wausau with his family the week before this scheduled weekend trip up north. He had left me with our dog, Mindy, when we broke up, but now that he had moved in with his family, Stephen said that he would take her back, as she needed more open spaces to run around in than I had. So Mindy was along on this trip as well.

The stop to drop off the dog in Wausau was awkward, to say the least. Even though Stephen wasn't there, it was difficult just seeing his mom and his younger brother, who were asking too many questions that couldn't be answered in front of my dad. I had not yet come out to my folks, though I had suspected for years that both of them already knew. I didn't talk about women in my life, and I wasn't bringing home any women I was supposedly seeing or dating. My folks had stopped asking about my social life many years before. We left Wausau and all those awkward questions, and, after a brief stop at the grocery store, we finally made it to the summer house late in the afternoon. I went ahead and made dinner in the 1930s kitchen that had only been slightly upgraded in the last forty years.

When dinner was ready, we sat down to eat at that rustic table in the dining area. The casual conversation between us was about our trip and how the house looked after the past winter. We also chatted about all of the raking we had to do to get the leaves away from the house and what needed to be done to open up the boathouse. Then, all of a sudden, the conversation made a decidedly sharp turn in the direction of a more serious and personal subject. It started by Dad asking questions about how I was doing after my breakup with my "roommate." He said that he and my mother wanted to know if I was doing okay. For some reason, as opposed to pulling on the straight mask as I had done for so many years, I just started opening up, answering his questions truthfully.

"Are you dating any women now?"

"Is your friend Roger gay?"

And then the big one: "Are you gay?"

I opened up without hesitation. No, I wasn't dating any women now. Yes, Roger was gay. And, "Yes, I am gay." The truthful answers kept falling out one after the other. It was liberating to finally open up.

Surprisingly, Dad took most of this in stride. That was unexpected because Dad was an accountant. Growing up with him, I learned that everything was either right or wrong, good or bad, and the figures either added up or they didn't. I had always believed that when the time came to tell him about my sexuality, he would give me more grief about it than my mom. Instead, he was very understanding and was very concerned about my well-being after the breakup.

That was twenty-one years ago. Until he died two years ago today, June 18, at age ninety-five, Dad didn't seem to care that I was gay. As he said, "I don't mind if you are gay, I just want you to be happy."

Over the remaining hours of that long weekend we spent together in 1985, opening up the house in Minocqua, we continued to talk, and I continued to open up to him. More questions and more truthful answers.

When we left Sunday morning, it was going to be a bright and sunny day. Already the sun, coming up on the other side of the lake, was streaming in through the windows we had uncovered. The opening up for another year was done. But this year, the opening-up ritual had taken on a whole new meaning for Dad and me. Not only had we opened the house for the coming summer months, but we had also opened up my life to him for the rest of his life.

A Psychic Made Me Do It

I CAME OUT nearly twenty-nine years ago. In 1977. During the summer of the Anita Bryant crisis. Because of a psychic.

It was at the wrap party for a PBS American Playhouse episode that we'd shot at Georgia's Foxfire Center and Museum, a place that has lovingly preserved the Southern Appalachian Mountain heritage and culture of the area's ancestors. I no longer remember the name of this particular episode, who starred in it, or even what job ETV had sent me there to perform, but I do remember vividly my disappointment when the psychic read my palm that night.

Now who knows why a psychic was even in attendance at that party on our last night in the beautiful mountains of northeast Georgia? She hadn't been part of the cast or crew, but I was pretty excited about it, having never actually met a psychic before. Her method of predicting the future was to read palms.

I was the last person in line, and, by the time she got around to me, she was clearly exhausted. I extended my palm to her with hopeful expectations of long life, wealth, and great love. She stared for a while at

14

my dainty-ish right hand joined to the girl-sized wrist I inherited from my mother, then sighed deeply and asked quietly, "Have you been up to the mountains to see Rabun Gap?" I told her, "No," and then she said, "Well, you really should go up there before you leave. It's beautiful."

And that was it.

Clearly, she was a phony, nothing more nor less than a one-woman tourist bureau.

But her words stuck with me, and, being in no particular hurry to get back to Columbia, I decided—what the hell, I'll probably never be here again, so why not drive up into the mountains for a look-see on the way home?

So, up and up, round and around I went, chugging along in the wonderful little blue VW Bug I eventually killed by stupidly driving it into the embankment at the end of Columbia's Wheat Street after another cast party a couple of years later. My advice to you? Don't drink and drive. But that's a commentary for another show.

After a Southern Baptist childhood of revivals and dreams of being a preacher (because he was the star of the show, I reckon), after small-town high school and a brief stint at the Citadel (and I won't bore you with all those gory details, except to say that I lasted five whole weeks longer than Shannon Faulkner, a feat I'm damned proud of), I enrolled at Limestone College, where my mother had graduated and where she'd met my father and where she and I had gone to classes together eighteen years earlier—I in her womb. In 1966, when I got there again, Limestone still had loose ties to the Southern Baptist Convention. Daily chapel was a requirement, as was a mandatory course in religion. The instructor was a brilliant biblical scholar; I went into class with my childhood belief system intact, and—to the chagrin of my Baptist family, and, no doubt, Limestone College—I emerged a semester later a much wiser man—a devout agnostic/sometime atheist—and happily remained a heathen for the next decade.

Until the day after that psychic casually suggested I go up into the mountains for a visit to Rabun Gap.

When I reached the top of the mountain, I pulled my VW Bug into a parking space, got out, and was overwhelmed by the magnificent view afforded by the Gap. For the first time in my life, I think I understood the line from "America the Beautiful" about "purple mountain majesties"—even though the Appalachian Mountains are verdant green in the summer, not purple like the ones out west.

From that majestic vantage point I could see what appeared to be an endless chain of giant mountains. In the valleys below, I could see the little people, my fellow humans, just about the size of ants, driving along in tiny cars, scurrying about, rushing to try to make some sense of their comparatively insignificant lives. And, for the first time in ten years—and certainly for the first time in my adult life—I realized there had to be a God. A Creator of all things large and small. And in that instant in the summer of 1977—at the same time when the orange juice queen and former Miss America Anita Bryant was proclaiming to the world that we homosexuals were evil—in that instant, I knew that this God had created me to be gay, and that this creation—gay little ol' me—was just as perfect a creation as the magnificent mountaintop on which I stood.

I was exhilarated, and forever grateful to my psychic tour guide. Had she foreseen my transformation into a suddenly self-accepting young gay man, my destiny somehow mysteriously encoded into the lines of my dainty palm? Or had she been, in fact, merely tired or bored—politely ending, as best she could, our brief encounter? I've no idea; only she and the God of the Mountaintop know for sure. While it amuses me to think that she accurately read my palm and my future, I do know this: I drove down the mountain to my mother's childhood home in Oconee County, found the graves of her parents—my grandparents, and came out to them first. The following week, I drove from Columbia to Gaffney to call an unheard-of Blanton family meeting and came out to my living relatives—my parents, my brother, and his first wife.

Sitting on the floor in front of them, I poured out my heart to them, crying most of the time, and introduced them to their real son and brother for the first time.

My mother looked straight at me for the entire two hours of my monologue, her eyes never leaving mine. My father stared at the floor. My brother, no doubt, held his breath the whole time, hoping the news wouldn't kill our parents. When I had no more tears left, my mother hugged me and told me she loved me, that her only concern was the difficulty I'd face in a world that didn't understand. My father made me promise to read the Bible. I agreed, providing he would read the books on homosexuality I'd brought home to try to help them understand. I don't really know, but I suspect he kept his promise to some extent; I didn't keep mine. But that June night in 1977, the night before Father's Day, whether he ever realized it or not, I gave him the best Father's Day gift he ever got. I gave him the gift of the real me.

Poor Daddy. That night we went to a wedding where all their friends kept asking, "When are *you* going to get married, Jimmy?" Newly out—but only just—I tried to smile and ignored the questions. And my dad was as pale as I ever saw him—at least until the cancer and the chemo took hold of him twenty-two years later.

Recently, I found a letter from my mother that I'd forgotten I had. She wrote it over the course of the week after that Father's Day that changed all our lives. The letter is full of agony—hers and Daddy's— but also suggests her deep love for her eldest son. There were beautiful letters from Dad and my brother, too, each in different ways coming to terms with their own "coming out" as the relative of a gay man. For a while, my family talked pretty often about my being gay. I was trying to force them into not just acceptance, but total gratitude for my God-given sexuality. Eventually, it became too exhausting to talk about, and we fell more or less into a mutual silence of knowledge and acceptance.

The events of that summer of '77, when my psychic tour guide pushed me to the mountaintop; when, a week later, I came out to my family; and, when—wonderfully!—Anita Bryant got a cream pie smashed into her pretty face and overly-coifed hair, causing her finally to shut the hell up—all those events made it possible for me, a lucky thirteen years later, on June 23, 1990, to march proudly down Main Street, Columbia, as the co-chair of South Carolina's first Pride March.

But that's another show.

Bernard Dewley

Highway 101

Plastic sacks
Bulging with T-shirts
And jeans
Knotted up tight
Two handfuls of AZT
Wrapped safe
In baggies
Stuffed in shoes

Everything at once
Crammed
In the back
Spilling down
The trunk twined shut
The dashboard creaking
Under the weight
Of dust
And a stack of poems
I scooped up
While
Charging into the wind
That bites my cheek

Squalls of rage
Warm my hand
As I flip on
The radio
And turn it
To the Oldies station
Low wattage AM
Crackling
But soothing

Round the corner
To Highway 101
Towards Gaffney
Maybe Nashville
I remember
My journal
Tucked
In the darkness
Of my brother's mattress
Hidden in the folds
Of the bed he'd OD'd in
But I push on

Under the cover
Of midnight willows
And crape myrtles
Just now blooming
I speed through these foothills
Inching closer to dawn
Barreling faster
Further
From here

By noon
I will be sore
From long hauling
Through mill towns
Over county line roads
Into new time zones
Past service stations
Clinging to *Cash Only* signs
Worn and yellowed
From two decades
Of sun and fumes

Hungry
I will stop
For biscuits and grits
Drop two dollars down
And crash into
Another town

Stacy Smallwood

Rainbows

so i'm in the car on i-64
with my mother and little cousin,
and he looks at the truck in front of us,
teal ford pickup,
fairly inconspicuous
and he asks me:
why does that guy have a rainbow
on his bumper?

i hear defcon 4 alerts in my head.
the painted lines on the highway
turn into tightropes.
i must walk this line very carefully,
especially with mom's heat vision
burrowing through the headrest.
etching the words "watch it"
on the back of my neck.

what can i tell him?
his eight-year-old mind might not be
ready for the truth:
that rainbows are reserved for those

who've made peace with sodom and gomorrah,
thrown leviticus out the window,
and vowed to abide by their own testament;
the gospel according to self.
that rainbows signify a pride
i don't yet possess
'cause even though mama knows,
i haven't really let her know she knows
and probably won't until i'm a lot more
financially and emotionally independent.

i look back at him,
his question still lingering in the air like dew,
waiting for the answer to settle on his ears.
i'm about to speak out when he spouts,
"i mean, rainbows are girlie things, right?"
again i sink into my seat
feeling like the reflectors i'm driving over
because i simply can't pay attention
to what lane i'm in.
and i in turn
think of my own questions like:
why have i only seen one black man
who ever had a rainbow on his car?
even in this era of black gay pride
where we parade around like lions,
baring our shaved chests
but afraid to show our scars,
proud of how we can fit one more passenger car
into those nightly trains,
while wrists are bound with thick black rope
fastened by the buckle of the bible belt.
are we afraid to dare to show our true colors,
thinking we'll bring disgrace to the family name,

tarnish that conservative Olympic bronze medal
that black folks treat like gold?
we might be first in our family to graduate from college,
own our own business,
fight for civil rights,
build our own home,
feed the hungry and homeless,
or even write poetry.
why should we feel ashamed of who we are
when we embody the very dreams of our ancestors?
why should we look at a positive HIV diagnosis
as God's way of punishing us for the lives we live in the dark?
rainbows are ribbons of light;
thin as vapor
but bold as the sun itself.
and they should not be reserved
for giant white polar bears, butch lesbians, and log cabin republicans
who can't pass for straight anymore.
where are the rainbows
for little black boys
whose compasses don't point north?

at the end of this personal sermon,
i open the doors to the church
and see my cousin standing there;
unfazed,
questioning,
and i think of his father
who may want the honor
of explaining his rainbow to him one day.
i think of my own
that i wear in my skin every day,
'cause when you blend all those colors together
brown is what you get.

so i speak up boldly
with a color in my voice
i didn't know i had
and say,
"no, rainbows aren't girlie;
they're strong
'cause you only see them come out
after you've weathered the storm."

Ed Madden

Gay Shame

ALTHOUGH WE LIKE TO TALK a lot about gay pride, let's admit, for a moment, that most of us live in a culture of shame. Indeed, we wouldn't have the phrase gay pride were it not for the fact that our culture is perpetually teaching us that being gay is something to be ashamed of. And we all make choices every day that reinforce that sense of shame.

The heater repairman comes in, and as I'm talking to him I think to myself, *Do I refer to my partner as my partner or my roommate?* I look around the house, wonder what he sees—the nude male painting, the copy of *The Advocate* on the table. I am simultaneously angry at myself for even thinking of these things. *It shouldn't matter,* I tell myself, *I'm out to my family, out at work. This is my home. It shouldn't matter.*

But for many of us, it does.

It's as if, for me, I'm perpetually stuck in ninth grade, my pants too short, my hand-me-down clothes out of date, my haircut dorky, and worse, realizing with total embarrassment that I am staring at the second-string quarterback in study hall, the beautiful boy with feathered hair, broad shoulders, and Topsiders. I'm aware that I can never name what I'm feeling—not just because of the constant homophobia of my high school culture, but also because of the more explicit messages about sexuality I'm getting from church and from my mother's growing involvement in right-wing politics. So I go home, close my bedroom door, put Evelyn Champagne King in the eight-track player, and sing along with that 1978 disco hit *Shame*, dancing in the mirror, my voice aching with hers as she sings, "Shame, / what you do to me is a shame / Mama just don't understand."

As we become aware of who we are, and as we act (or don't act) on that knowledge, we do so in a culture that both condemns homosexuality and denies it through silence, as if it were something so deeply shameful it can't be talked about. And we learn to participate in the very silence that reinforces our sense of shame and isolation.

How many gay and lesbian people fill out forms and check the box "single" even though they have been living with the same person for decades? How many gay and lesbian people censor their conversations at work, lying—or lying through omission—about their identities, their families, and their lives? How many gay men speak contemptuously of drag queens or effeminate men as the ones who ruin it for the rest of us? What decisions do we make that reinforce a culture of shame?

In a recent *USA Today* article, a gay television producer said that gay and lesbian actors should come out. "When you stay in the closet," he said, "you perpetuate a culture of shame. It's about personal courage and integrity." That may be true. But in the same article, the actors who described sabotaged or stagnant careers made it clear that these choices are neither easy nor without consequence.

I don't want to dismiss the very real risks and fears many of us have. Nor do I want to make light of the ways shame cripples us. After years of volunteering at the Harriet Hancock Community Center, I've heard too many stories about people losing their jobs, fighting for custody of their children, or being assaulted. And having been someone who wrote anti-gay newspaper editorials in college, denying my own sexuality by attacking others, I am deeply aware of the ways shame distorts and destroys.

When we talk about gay pride, we need to think seriously about the ways we perpetuate gay shame, not just those who are in the closet but those of us who claim to be out and proud as well. In the extraordinary book *Coming Out of Shame* by Gershen Kaufman and Lev Raphael, the authors say that coming out only partially breaks the cultural hold of shame on our lives. We still live with its effects.

As they say, shame is at work in the silence within our own families around our being gay. It may inform our lack of political consciousness and drive our addictive behaviors. And it is also apparent in the ways we attack other gay people. How many of us internalize our shame in crippling ways—from depression and denial to addictive behaviors or perfectionism? How many of us externalize our shame by projecting it, transferring our own sense of blame and contempt onto other gay and lesbian people?

Pride marches—those moments of community empowerment and celebration and indeed pride—are themselves often microcosms of the social and personal dynamics of shame. There is the closeted man on the sidewalk, following the march but not walking in it, as well as the kid who reacts to the shame of the closet by decking himself in everything rainbow. The business person who complains about the embarrass-ment of drag queens and leather, and the activist whose political work compensates for family rejection. The march itself may be framed by the discreet family picnic that offers community without public outness and by gay pride events in other, larger cities. How many South Caro-linians go to Pride in Atlanta or Charlotte but refuse to participate in or support local pride events, where their participation might involve more risk but also have more impact?

We need to recognize and talk honestly with each other about the complicated ways we live with, react to, internalize, and perpetuate a culture of gay shame, both sexual and social. There are no easy answers. Just bring up the topic of being out at work at your next gay dinner party, and you'll see these are also not easy discussions.

A friend of mine was recently featured in *The State* newspaper, in a section profiling a number of young community leaders. His profile stood out. There, under the category Family, he had written, "My partner of six years." We all make choices at moments like that. For many of us, the choice to name a partner in such a public context would be a difficult one. We would ask what might be at risk, how will others react? We would imagine that morning, opening the newspaper, and seeing for the first time in black and white a public confession of who and what we are. We might feel all over again the shame washing over our bodies. *Shame, / I wouldn't want to live with the pain. / Mama just don't understand.*

When I emailed him to thank him, he wrote me back, "I didn't even think about it. [My partner] is my family." I wish we could all react the same way, but we can't. Yet.

What decisions do we make—because of fear or economics or family or risks, both imagined and real—that reinforce a culture of shame? Andrew Holleran once wrote, "Only by dealing with Gay Shame will we ever get to a definition of Gay Pride." That is, only by examining our own personal and cultural shame will we be able to assert gay pride in a way that is more than an annual march and more than a glib slogan.

Melissa Gainey

Torn

THE STARS WERE OUT. Shifting uncomfortably on a torn Oklahoma State blanket, I glanced sideways at the person gazing upward to my left. The outline of her spiky white hair was a silhouette made by the perfect round moon above us, and I suppressed a laugh as I thought of Maggie Simpson. I was fourteen. She was eighteen. We were not supposed to be friends.

I met her walking through Columbia, South Carolina's annual Mayfest—a drunken, redneck celebration of the beginning of weather tame enough for spaghetti straps and Wrangler "Daisy Dukes." I giggled with my group of mascara-clad, stoned girlfriends, pointing out cute guys and talking shit to girls who thought they were tougher than us. Honestly, I don't think many of them were. We were country girls—girls with scars on our knuckles and deep in our souls. Girls with no daddies or daddies who beat them, or replacement, drug-addicted daddies that called us by the wrong names. We were all truant, we were all angry, and we all wanted to have a damned good time and do it on whatever drug was available.

I was nothing like this inside, but gave an Oscar-deserving performance that eventually bled into my true character. We passed by a
group of big girls who were laughing uncontrollably. The rest of my
clan sauntered by, staring hard, but I stopped, recognizing a purple-
haired giant named Michelle who had been in my remedial math class.
We spoke and she introduced me to my first nightmare. "Do you want
to come to our barbeque tomorrow night?" "Sure."

I fell in love with Deb on that torn Oklahoma State blanket in her
front yard. It was a suburban neighborhood with white fences and tiny
dogs walked by little old ladies and the rich wives of lawyers. We had
been lying there for hours, talking about my family. This was a subject
normally reserved for my therapist and my poetry book, but it came
out of my mouth like a dam broken, splashing into her attentive ears. I
feared she might drown. At the end of my story she took my face in her
hands and stared into my eyes like a child that had just been reunited
with its mother.

It was a stare I cannot forget, no matter how many years I have
avoided her eyes. I asked her what she was thinking. She kissed me. It
was as if the broken shards of glass inside of me floated toward each
other, meeting at my stomach and making their way out of me—out of
the wet, sick darkness that had churned for so long. The pieces scattered
down that exquisitely smooth blacktop and found their way into some
other lost child's body. I felt sorry for them for the moment but was
relieved that they were gone.

My life in hiding began on that blanket. For the next three years I
would learn to lie as if my breath depended on it. And to be a pretty
girl from South Congaree, where the words "Baptist" and "faggot" were
used with almost the same regularity, I sometimes believed it actually
did. My mother was irate that any of my time was spent with "those
weird girls" and she eventually prohibited me from seeing "them." So I
got a boyfriend. His name was Jessie and he was a beautiful, energetic,
hilarious gay boy who clapped his hands and jumped in the air screaming, "Brilliant! You are f-ing brilliant!" when I proposed the idea to
him. We grinned for the prom pictures and left to meet our lovers at the
Embassy Suites. Popping champagne we toasted to our lifelong loves.

May we one day get married and have beautiful, screaming, shitting, snotty babies so our parents will love us.

Eventually, the novelty of being secretive wears off. It is like an affair. It is exciting and new and thrilling and naughty and all of a sudden, it is just normal. This is usually the point where the husband crawls back to the wife. But I had my wife. I had nowhere to crawl except further inside of myself. Deb had become extremely abusive. She blamed it on being forced to hide. She blamed it on my immaturity. She blamed it on her mental illness. She blamed and I cried, and she left and I died. She slit her wrists and I punched out my windshield and she overdosed. Then we did it all over again.

I began to fail classes. I screamed at my sister and threw things and stayed gone as much as I could. When I was home, my mother looked at me with cold, clear understanding. I did not try to talk about Jessie. I was too tired to pretend. She knew what was happening to me and because she could not accept it, she could not help me. I heard other girls whimpering in the gazebo at lunchtime about how Chet or Bret or Kevin had broken up with them and how their mothers did things like take them shopping or rub their heads or tell them stories of their first heartbreaks and "Honey, you don't know this now, but it will be okay" and hand them money for the movies. My mother's hand offered me nothing but a firm grip on my hair and a slap across the face when she woke up without her Vicadin.

I began to sit in my room for hours, writing feverishly, ripping out pages and sobbing uncontrollably. She heard me. I made sure of it. Never was there a knock at my door. And there never would be.

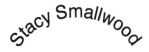
Stacy Smallwood

Mother's Day

as a child, i remember mother's back
beneath my feet,
crushing her tension into wine
between my toes,
hoping this would help her sleep deeper
and wake up more flesh than granite.
i worried about breaking her,
that my feet might find a fault
along the line of her spine
and split her,
but she reassured me
bearing me on her back is what a mother is built for.

so i kept walking,
moving mountains beneath my heels
to give her some relief,
amazed at this steel strength glowing
under my soles,
but unwilling to share the weight of my difference with her
even though i knew at that young age.

last night, under a warm spring moon, i met another woman
whose back was cast in titanium and iron.
a woman named harriet hancock.
an entire state came out to thank her
for helping to organize south carolina's first pride march
fifteen years ago,
digging hands in dying earth
commanding it to bear rainbow fruit,
fighting death threats and legislators,
helping men to leave the sewers
and dance in the glory of sun
on one saturday morning every year,
all because her son had the courage to say
"i'm gay."

i can only imagine how the blood erupted in his face
when he turned to tell her,
forcing seas to swell and spill over his eyes
as he squeezed the words out of his gut,
how his muscles wove like rope to hang him
as he stood before the only person his face could never lie to,
how he ground his teeth into salt that dissolved in his mouth
and burned a tongue that would rather roll into his lungs
and hide until danger passed
than confess his sins to one who had already forgiven him.

two words
that inspired a woman
to change the world.

And this is what i want for you, mother;
a broken but complete son to love,
with as few shadows as possible
and an honest tongue.
but how do i tell you,

the woman who always said "don't you ever bring
    a white woman home to me"
that i'd rather bring a black man instead?
how do you wrap that in a ribbon and say "happy mother's day"?

but this is what i bring home to you,
stomach knotted, knees weak,
butterflies and chainsaws in flux.
but i need to stand on your back again,
want you to know the comfort
of your son's naked feet
digging and burying secrets where he knows
they'll be safe,
hoping your body won't reject them.
maybe you'll cry under the weight
the same way i have,
or maybe you'll tense your muscles
and erode me out of your soil,
or maybe you'll find the cause
you were never searching for,
a reason to post a parade down gatesville's only street,
a whole new way to love your broken child back together
and tell him it's okay,
that God doesn't make mistakes.
perhaps you'll lie to me and tell me i'm perfect
just as i am,
and i might believe it.
but i'm so scared now,
scared to turn the only woman i've ever loved
against me
scared to confirm her greatest christian fears,
scared to watch her steel melt around my ankles,
praying my answers to her questions
could become her cause
and not my crucifix.

Slipper Socks

Valentine's Day 2006

HE MAY HAVE BEEN A MYTH, but St. Valentine has oddly stuck with Americans who can scarce let a month pass without some holiday or the other to remind us how hopelessly kitschy we can—and like—to be. The poorer will head to Eckerd or CVS and hope that one last sampler box has not been snapped away, while the wealthier will head to some coffee shoppe and brandish a Godiva box all the way to the wrap stand, probably making sure the overhead light catches the foil so all the peons can behold.

Flowers will be just as ubiquitous, assembled by an army of tired florists who have assumed the almost priestly function of wrapping twelve-count overpriced absolutions offered up to gloss a multitude of yearly sinning. Or they might be vain hopes in dull-green tissue paper overdressed in jungle-red glitter. And everyone will be secretly grouchy. Sins of the world are not easy to bear, much less bundle up in baby's breath. Still, we cheerfully buy the indulgences under the benign gaze of this de-sainted saint, pretending somehow that the whole jingling-change mess is for the benefit of someone else's soul and not our own.

35

Personally, I will be in the CVS crowd. It's where you find the slipper socks the old ladies wear, because the memory of slipper socks, of all ridiculous things, is one of the most potent reminders of what love actually is, at least as I have known and been graced by it.

I was so very young when I drove to that house in Weatherford, Texas. I had just started practicing law, my post in a town dominated by the gloomy sag of a Second Empire courthouse built by the cattle barons when their dreams were measured in horns, hooves, and hard gold eagles. Like many houses in every town just like Weatherford, it was well kept, its mistress an obviously house-proud matron who—no doubt—had the blue rinse every Monday and sang in some choir every Sunday. And this was so. The prim woman who answered the door was indeed a cheerful stereotype who welcomed me graciously even though my briefcase held her son's living will. And I noticed she wore slipper socks.

A bad, bad sign.

Such women, even when ill themselves, do not meet strangers on business in sock feet. Their padding across the pleasantly dowdy living room towards the small garage converted into a sickroom spoke of haste, energies that could not be wasted in something as mundane as putting on shoes. Her feet told me that time was fleeting.

He lay there in a steel-framed, medical-supply-house bed, diapered with akimbo arms, the only thing vital in his wasteland body, so unlike his body and face flaring out of the past in a picture she had propped on his bedside table. Another man also floated out of this picture, equally handsome, memory from days when "gym bodies" and "manscaping" still slept in some Madison Avenue parvenu's imagination. He had his arms draped around him, their twin belt buckles looking to Eastern eyes like plates hammered in wild, barbarian gold.

She sat. She listened to me explain what the paper in my case meant, allowed me to loan her my pen. She held it up to his hand, moving his gaunt fingers with her own into the broad, swooping loops that had once spelled his name, not hers. Women like this, from her time, wrote in copperplate. Not the defiant lariats of the educated cowboy.

I sealed the paper on the lid of the corner washing machine after I pushed aside the vase filled with Texas roses she had placed there, probably to drive away the dry smells that come when Death has His way and, job almost done, waits to be called to His supper. I gave her the paper, accepted the kind invitation to a cup of coffee in the kitchen. After she washed his face and kissed him, I followed her out, stopping to see that, while I had been busy about my grisly work, she had slipped on shoes.

Her son, because of one little piece of paper, was no longer in danger of maybe getting stuck, inhabiting some terrible twilight between death and life. It was a sanctified bargain, legal, marked by the drying ink and the handshake her son no longer had the strength to give. In the space of a small time and one signature, the definition of time itself had somehow changed. Coffee could now be brewed and easy hospitality extended. She could adjust the picture on the bedside table, and her son's eyes could see the man he loved and lost before deciding to follow.

And we were alone. The kitchen was stuffed with dishes of nameless good things Southerners like to bring to the dead and dying—although if it is to banish death with the stuff of life or to placate an angry ghost to be, I cannot say. But they were dishes brought by phantom hands. I do not think it mattered to her. I doubt it, anyway. If she resented her son being borne and buried by those selfsame phantom food-bringers or eulogized by some backcountry pastor who mouths of Heaven but relishes Hell, she did not say. Her child was sleeping in the garage. Sound carries on hot, quiet afternoons.

The temptation is to see them as pieta, a living tableaux of memory from a time gay people don't fondly recall, as no one fondly remembers any red season of dying. But the pieta is a disservice, and I think they would have resented the comparison as blasphemous. It was enough that she greeted me at her door in slipper socks, putting aside her own life and upbringing for the sake of the comfort of another, someone who bore well-wishers who, I imagined, glanced at the garage entry door and made crippled excuses for not going inside. It was enough that she gave her child an unashamed picture and a last gift of writing his name for him as close to his hand as she could come.

Have candy, have flowers. Enjoy the goofy fun of courtship and even the weird fun of not being able to land the object of desire. But this year, perhaps spare a thought for something small and hidden speaking to only two people who love, whomever they are, small things like wearing slipper socks when the stranger knocks. This is how love is defined for one another, and flourishes, even in acid soil. As the Texas roses do.

Becci Robbins

For John, at Christmas

Christmas 2005

"HE HAS FULL-BLOWN AIDS," she said. The sound of it like air escaping.
Full. Blown. AIDS.

The social worker handed over his file, a single sheet of paper scrawled with handwritten notes, mostly addresses and phone numbers, which I scanned for clues to what might be coming.

She said John was forced to leave his home in Los Angeles after becoming too ill to care for himself. He had moved in with his sister, who was stationed at Fort Jackson, but it was not an ideal living arrangement. She was often gone; he was increasingly bedridden. She had an alcohol problem; he had a drug habit. She resented the intrusion in her life; he, in turn, was humiliated, lonely, and raging mad.

After being left alone for three days, John called Palmetto AIDS Life Support Services in Columbia to ask that someone be sent over to make sure he didn't "starve to freakin' death." As a PALSS volunteer, that was to be my job—to make sure he didn't "starve to freakin' death."

It was early fall when I first met John. He was just forty-one but looked decades older. He was stooped, bent into sharp angles of elbows and knees. His skin was transparent, shot through with a stringy pattern of bruise-colored veins. There was a lesion on his face. Another on his neck. I tried not to stare. He had a watery gaze, his pale eyes rimmed with loose, red lids, which he blinked the way he did everything else—slowly, deliberately.

From our first meeting I knew that it wasn't starving to death that worried John; he was afraid of disappearing. My job was simply to reflect him back, to be his witness.

In November, John was released from the hospital so he could go home for Thanksgiving. It was his last chance to reconnect with his family in ways they never had. His hope was that they all might come together as a real family—for him—for once. His fantasy was that his mother and father, seeing that their son was dying, would reach out and gather him in.

But John's parents—stunned by their son's garish disease—had nothing to say, nothing to give, not even the customary peck on the cheek.

The trip exhausted him. He was crushed by his parents' chilly reception and drained by the strain of travel. By Christmas, he was close to the edge, wishbone-thin and haunted by hallucinations.

Slowly, he began to turn inside. Entire visits he would spend with his face to the wall. More and more, he began to talk about God. The deeper he spiraled into his illness, the more useless I felt. I no longer spoke his language. He no longer lived in my world. On one of my last visits he said, "I'm not afraid of dying—I'm afraid of this."

This: a room on the sixth floor of Providence Hospital. Stale air. The incessant hum of machines. Strangers' voices outside in the hall. Nurses moving about his room, putting tubes in his arms, notes in his chart, changing the channels on TV. "I hate this," he said, and with all the strength trapped in his tight body, he threw his dinner tray against the wall. Chicken bones splayed out across the linoleum. Pearls of tapioca slid down the back of the door.

Surprised by his own theatrics, John started to laugh, and then howl. Satisfied by his tantrum, he demanded a cigarette. To my raised eyebrow, he snapped, "What's it going to do, kill me?"

It was late and against the rules but I loaded him into a chair and wheeled him into the elevator. We went down to the outside courtyard, gray and slick with a misting rain, where he smoked and told stories until the cold drove us back inside. On the way back to his room, we stole from the empty lobby all the poinsettias that would fit on his lap. We lined them along his window sill, where they fluttered and wilted in the rising heat.

John's final venture outside the hospital was for Christmas Eve at Trinity Episcopal Cathedral. For weeks he talked about little else. Against his doctor's advice, he was released from the hospital for the evening.

He arrived at the church wrapped in a long, black coat and a very purple scarf. As he made his way down the aisle, he was radiant. With intense, burning eyes, John took it all in: the candles, the choir, the stained glass, the carved wood, the faces around him soft in prayer. We crushed into a pew together and I reached for his hand. I could feel the blood pumping under his tissue-paper skin.

Halfway through the service, John excused himself to go the restroom. When he didn't return, we assumed he had stayed at the back of the church. Only later did we discover that he had collapsed on the bathroom floor, where he waited, helpless, while listening to the congregation sing songs of praise.

The last time I saw John, he didn't know I was there. It was January, the dead of winter. He was incoherent, drenched in sweat, curled into a question mark. I sat by his bed and waited for him to come back. I studied his face. Matched my breathing to his. I wandered to the window and looked into the empty courtyard. I ate the lemons from his night stand. I watched him and I waited.

I wondered whether the trips he took were in his head or somewhere across the universe, or were those places one and the same? I never got to ask him. John died that night, alone in his private room.

That was fifteen years ago now but my memories of John remain sharp. They come to me at odd times, but more often during the holidays, which he loved. That the last trip outside the hospital was on Christmas Eve strikes me as a measure of God's grace, a final gift to a dying man whose faith was failing him just when he needed it most.

John's gift to me was an expanded awareness, of time, of beauty, of family, of community, of the journey toward death each of us walks every day. That perspective has served me well. So thank you, John, for letting me in and for letting me bear witness. And, wherever you are, Merry Christmas.

Ed Madden

The Bridge That Has Fallen In

Thanksgiving 2007

ON THE WAY TO LUNCH TODAY, I walked past a lone tree I often pass in the parking lot. The tree is ridding itself of leaves, revealing masses of mistletoe, gleaming dark green in the cold air. I've never noticed them before—in the summer they disappear in the rustling oak—but here they are, and soon that's all there'll be, just clouds of dark green gleaming in the bare branches.

At lunch, we talk about the holidays. "The buildup is so incredible," says my friend Doak. "There can't be anything but disappointment." His favorite holiday memory, he says, is coming home from a Christmas service at the cathedral, pouring a toddy, sitting down and admiring the tree his partner Gordon and their girls decorated—and listening, he says, to the quiet.

Yesterday I sent cards to distant family who will not reply. I am thinking that there are many ways of measuring distance, geography only the most obvious. I am thinking that we create families in many ways—blood and love not always the same thing.

I am reminded of this every Thanksgiving. I spend part of the day at lunch with my partner's sister and her children, a raucous bunch who have made me one of their own. I spend dinner with a growing group of dear friends. And I spend too much of the day longing for a family I haven't seen in years. Though I celebrate the holidays with Bert's family and with our friends, some part of me wants to return to a home in Arkansas where I am neither accepted nor, I suspect, welcome.

I remember what it was like when I was in college, out at school and totally closeted at home. I stayed in Austin for Thanksgiving, attending a large and welcoming lesbian potluck where a poem from Walt Whitman was the prayer of choice. But on Christmas I drove the twelve-hour drive home. For several years, I developed painful stomach cramps while I was home. My mother said—somewhat jokingly, somewhat sadly—that she hoped they weren't making me sick. My doctor said the problem was related to stress. I knew it was a symptom of the closet. I couldn't speak about things important to me—my boyfriend, my gay-friendly church, even my research in gay and lesbian literature. It was as if my body physically enacted my attempts to stifle and watch my conversation, my whole body in a vicious clench of silence.

Last year at Thanksgiving, my friend Susan suggested that we go around the table and talk about the things we are thankful for. We didn't do it, but we did instead raise a heartfelt toast to the hosts and to our friendship. And beside me, raising his glass of red wine, holding my hand, and smiling that sweetly goofy smile I adore, was the man I love.

This weekend I will sit at my sister-in-law's table, eat her holiday ham and my partner's delicious bourbon chocolate pecan pie. I won't go home. And yet there is some part of me that imagines driving down that long gravel road to the family farm and up to my childhood home, a ranch house surrounded by mulberry trees, the combines rumbling through the fields nearby.

The old wooden bridge I used to drive across has fallen in; no one drives that way anymore. And I know the interstate has finally made it to my hometown—only another ten minutes out to the farm. But that fallen bridge has cut off the road that goes through the farm, leaving my childhood home on a dead-end road.

The days are getting colder. The yard fills with leaves, and any day now, winter will descend on South Carolina. Near my building at school, the Bradford pears are like something from Willie Wonka, the supple leaves of butterscotch and cherry and peach sorbet giving way to a brittle but rich chocolate brown. I am thinking about the way this season throws things into relief, like mistletoe gleaming in a bare tree.

As I walk back to my office from lunch with Doak, I pause to admire the mistletoe, unreachable. Soon we'll be dragging out the Christmas decorations, the cold weather clothes—those lambskin gloves, left to Bert by a friend who died of AIDS. I remember my father, in a fit of bitterness, returned his Christmas presents several years ago, unopened—a flannel shirt, brown gloves, a book. I have Christmas cards stacked and ready to write. On the refrigerator there's a photo of a nephew I've never met, a niece I've never seen. Bert's sister's ham will be salty and sweet, and his pecan pie will be, as always, delicious. I won't go back. Those bare branches in the parking lot will display a beautiful and gleaming green. Those old gloves from a friend will keep me warm.

Linda Ketner

The Death of My Friend

I'M WRITING FROM MY HOMETOWN of Salisbury, North Carolina. I drove up for the funeral of a woman who has been my friend since second grade. Long friendships such as ours are irreplaceable, and the planet feels lonely without her tonight.

When I moved from Raleigh to Salisbury in the second grade, her desk was beside mine in Mrs. Eudy's room. I was terrified in this new school and obviously fighting back tears throughout the morning. She would alternately send me reassuring looks followed by juggling acts or clown faces to try to make me laugh.

When recess came, she was captain of one of the kickball teams. She picked me first. "I'll take Ketner!" she said. "I'll bet you're really good at kickball, Ketner!" As I passed, she thrust a lint-covered Oreo at me from her pocket.

If you've ever been lonely and petrified as a child, you know what a gift she gave me. My fear was gone. I had a friend. It was the first of many gifts I received from her—as did everyone who knew her.

We went through twelve years of school and four years of college together. Brownies, Girl Scouts, Mrs. Carter's ballroom dancing, Girls State, sleepovers, school plays, clubs, sports—she was in the fabric of much of my early life. And, although she was everyone's best friend, she didn't date much in high school or college. She was plenty attractive. She just felt like the guys' best friend and not someone they would think to ask out.

Fast forward through her job in government—my marriage and divorce and acceptance of my sexuality—and you'll find us in the car together on the way to the city park for our fifteenth-anniversary high school reunion. Although I had been in a relationship for five years, I was still in the closet, so I was tap dancing my brains out trying to avoid lying to her when she'd ask questions about my life! I'd dodge and volley questions back at her. Back and forth we went in this elaborate non-conversation until the light bulb went off in my head! I screeched the car to a halt, turned to her and yelled, "Are you a lesbian?!"

Her mouth fell open and she gave me the stunned-mullet look and said, "Jeeezus! What the hell kind of question is that?!! Good Lord, I can't believe you! What in the world ... "

I interrupted with, "'Cause I am!"

Many "omigods" later, we collapsed in laughter, relief, and connection.

All night long we traded double entendres while we made our way through the reunion events. Finally, we were able to sit in the car and talk until three a.m. about our real lives and the people in it. We could retrace high school and look beneath our always-smiling, good-girl images to the truth of our young selves. And the truth was full of high school crushes on female teachers and "best friends," of bottled-up feelings, guilt, fear, isolation, and heartache. We traded some pretty silly questions—"If you could date any movie star, who would it be?" Things we could have, should have, done in high school, but never had the chance.

We stayed in touch over the passing years. She lost a long-term relationship because she wasn't willing to come out of the closet. I left a long-term relationship in part because my partner wasn't willing to come out of the closet. We talked much about the closet during those days. It boiled down to my saying I had to come out—that I couldn't stand the lying and the distance it created in all of my relationships. She said she had to stay in—that it would kill her parents, and she would lose all of her straight friends. We didn't try to change each other's minds, we just each wanted to be understood.

Tomorrow, we will bury my buddy—and her secret with her. Only two of the five hundred people at her funeral will truly know who she was. I haven't mentioned her name here because of that. You see, I respect her privacy even in death—until she tells me otherwise.

She was deeply loved. But only two of us in the church will know who she loved.

How many of us will die with only two people knowing our deepest loves, our truest selves before this idiocy toward LGBT people is over? How long will this stupid, life-draining bigotry go on? How many of us, for how long, will think we need to protect the people we love from the good and decent people we are?

My friend was loveable and good, all of her. And now—finally—she is sure of it.

I celebrate your truest, dearest self, my friend. I thank God that I didn't choose your lonely road. I fight on so that this dimming and diminishment of lives as beautiful as yours will come to an end.

Help us from the other side with a metaphoric Oreo—I know you will.

Candace Chellew-Hodge

Out at the State Fair

In 2005, the South Carolina Equality Coalition sponsored a booth at the South Carolina State Fair. It was the first such public outreach on behalf of gay and lesbian families. Volunteers staffing the booth distributed equality bracelets and information about an upcoming amendment that would prohibit marriages, civil unions, and other protections for these couples and their children. This amendment later passed in 2006.

MY PARTNER WANDA and I had a great Friday night at the state fair. Within our first fifteen minutes we had at least four positive interactions with people. The bracelets drew them in and after that it was just a matter of giving them our speech.

Most of the people who approached the table were completely unaware of the amendment, but once told about it they weren't surprised that it would happen in South Carolina. People are also very confused about which way to vote if they want to defeat the amendment. I kept stressing "vote NO next November."

I would say that ninety-nine percent of our interactions through the night were very, very positive. I learned not to judge book by its cover—ever. One very redneck-looking man almost ran up to the booth, grabbed a few bracelets and asked, "May I have these?" "Sure," I said, "but you have to hear my pitch." He smiled broadly, "I don't have to hear your pitch, two of my family members are gay and I'll vote against anything that hurts them." I wanted to hug him.

Then, two African-American sisters poked through the bracelets and chatted with me. One was the mother of a twenty-six-year-old lesbian, the other the adoring aunt.

"I don't want my daughter to face any discrimination," the mom told me, and the aunt emphatically agreed.

One lily-white couple with the appropriate 2.5 children stopped to chat and thought the amendment was a terrible idea. They said they'd certainly vote no.

A man with a military-style haircut stopped by with his three kids and wife in tow and was adamant about voting against the amendment. He was angry over Westboro Baptist Church leader Fred Phelps and his recent protests of the funerals of soldiers killed in Iraq. He was all for fairness—for us and for soldiers.

One experience that could have been negative turned positive. An older white man and his wife stopped by and talked for a long while with Wanda. (I was talking with others but joined the conversation late.) In the first part of the conversation, he told Wanda he was undecided but leaning toward voting for the amendment. His wife disagreed. After Wanda explained the amendment further, he began to hem and haw a bit.

"Well, I'm a Christian..." he began.

"So are we!" we chimed in.

A pained expression crossed his face.

"I'm a minister," I offered with a smile.

His grimace grew deeper and he waved off the comment. "I'm not even going to get into that," he shook his head, but continued, "I'm a Christian and God tells me to love everybody, so even if I don't agree, I still have to love everyone."

Wanda told me this man told her he was raised in a racist home, and if someone was gay and he was in the same room with them, he'd leave. Now, he says, he has gay friends and they're all right with him.

By the time he walked away, he had decided to vote against the amendment.

One lady made her children return the bracelets telling them, "You can't have those. They're lesbians!" Whatever.

The bottom line of all the positive experiences—these people either had family members or friends who were gay. What came home to me is the absolute importance for people to be out! It makes such a difference to other people to know gay people and understand our lives.

Lauren Wiggins

Total Little Lesbian

I WAS IN MY USUAL SPOT on the stairs at recess, eavesdropping on teacher talk. I had taken to getting into trouble rather than subjecting myself to being shunned by the girls on the monkey bars or being rejected from playing soccer with the boys. Usually, the teachers would talk about their husbands or other boring stuff. Sometimes I would hear some good gossip about one of the kids they had to send to the principal's office.

As I sat there in my suspenders, pulling at the end of my new tie and waiting for the bell to ring, I heard the word. It was the voice of my homeroom teacher: "Total little lesbian." I looked over and caught them all staring at me. They quickly turned, some giggled, and someone started a new discussion.

I was seven years old and I didn't have a clue about the meaning of the word. After recess, I asked to go to the library. I needed answers and I figured a dictionary would help. I strolled down the fiction aisle and perused the magazine rack, careful not to look anxious. Fearing a wandering librarian might expose my agenda, I checked out a book on reptiles and headed for the door. Here it was, the moment of truth, contained in the oversized dictionary a mere ten feet from the exit. I'd flip a page, scan it, look up to make sure no one noticed me.

Was I sweating? Was my hand shaking? Did I already know what the word meant? Finally, my eye caught *lesbian*, but the definition only talked about being from the island of Lesbos. The only island I knew of was Hawaii. Then I saw that there was an "ism." Lesbianism. It sounded like a disease, but the definition said that it had to do with "homosexual behavior" between women. Unsure of the exact definition of homosexual but aware of its connotation, I flipped to the "H" section. I began to piece it all together.

I went to the restroom immediately, pocketed my tie, slipped my shirt over my suspenders. I had barely been able to sleep the night before, thinking about wearing my new clothes. I even picked out my whole outfit and modeled it for my mom, including the perfect socks. Now I didn't even want to go back to class. I felt ashamed; no one else was a lesbian. I was sure that the tie and suspenders were to blame. Tomorrow would be different. If Mommy could buy me a dress to wear for picture day next week, then no one would suspect me of being one of those. There would be pictures: proof that I was just a regular girl. I could give them to my favorite teachers to display on their filing cabinets. Then everyone would be sure I wasn't a lesbian. So I dug a hole on the side of our apartment building and put my accessories to rest. R.I.P grey and red paisley, clip-on tie. R.I.P black suspenders with shiny silver clips.

After picture day had come and gone, I hadn't heard the word in some time. Then, on field day, none of the girls wanted to be tied to me for the three-legged race. I was never first pick, but it was widely known that Lauren Wiggins was an asset to any kickball team during P.E. So was it because we had to be tied together that no one wanted to be my partner? When I asked my teacher what I was supposed to do, she looked at the other girls and then back at me. They all seemed to be exchanging glances in a code that I could not decipher. Finally, she said that she would trade me with someone who had a single-person event. The good news was that I took first place in the fifty-yard dash. The bad news was that I felt an indescribable shame for the next twelve years from that incident, a feeling that could never be repressed. It was a disenchantment that would sporadically pounce on me and nearly drive me in the ground deeper than I had buried that stupid tie and those dorky suspenders. It no longer mattered what I wore because now everything in my closet seemed to bear the label that would cause me to resent, so much for so long.

Not anymore though. I've since found other girls who really like my ties.

Tinabeth

"VIVIAN AND JL MCCUNE ARE MOVING into the McGinnis house this week," Ma said. "JL has gotten a job at the pump station so they're coming back to Richards."

Ma, my grandmother on my daddy's side, was passing the little plate of fried cornbread to me and talking to Pa. They liked to fill each other in on any news when he came home from the barbershop for lunch every day. I took two pieces of the cornbread and handed it to Pa.

Lunch at my grandparents' house in the summer was always delicious. Today we had fresh white cream peas, sliced tomatoes that had come from Mrs. Lee's garden, cucumber salad with vinegar and sugar soaking the onions and cucumbers, fried okra, and corn on the cob drenched in butter. We ate in the kitchen at a small, round table that had a definite head: my grandmother.

She ruled the table and the rest of our lives with an iron will and irrepressible wit. My grandfather understood his role and laughed at everything she said. He didn't rule anything except his barbershop.

"And the best news is that they have two daughters that you can play with, Sheila Rae," Ma continued. "Tinabeth will be in the first grade when school starts, and Sarah Katherine is a year younger. You know I've been wanting you to have some other little girls to play with. You spend entirely too much time running with the boys, riding horses, and playing baseball. Once these girls move in, we'll go right over there and say hello. I always liked Vivian when they lived here before. I never did believe all of that talk about how much whisky she drank. Did you, George?"

"Well, no, I guess I just never thought that much about it," Pa said.

"Exactly. That's your tendency, so I have to keep up with everything," Ma said, and then made a grand sweeping gesture that implied that her kingdom required much of her.

"I don't like playing with girls. They're never any fun. All they want to do is talk and pretend. Butch and Rush and I have a secret club with no girls allowed. We have rules and everything." I didn't add that I couldn't possibly be interested in any girls who were so much younger than me. After all, I was going to be in the second grade. These new girls were babies.

"You might as well make up your mind to going with me day after tomorrow," Ma said with a frown. Then she softened. "I'm frying up some pineapple pies to take with us. How does that sound to you?"

Now we're getting somewhere, I thought. Maybe it was a good idea to visit the new neighbors, after all.

Two days later, Ma and I drove over to the McCune's house with a basket full of pineapple pies. As a bribe, Ma had given me several to take home after letting me sample one. Her kitchen had smelled so sweet from cooking the pies that I could have eaten all of mine right then, but she'd said one was enough for now.

Ma had also made me take off my holsters and six-shooters that I was playing with before we left. She asked where the doll was that she had given me last Christmas. I told her I didn't know for sure. She just shook her head.

"You need to be playing with little girl things," she said. "Why your daddy and granddaddy encourage you to be a tomboy is beyond me."

I wanted to please Ma, but it was hard to know what to say sometimes. I should have been a boy, I thought. Then it wouldn't be so confusing.

Ma stopped the car and we got out. We really could have walked here, but Ma never walked anywhere. Why walk when you can ride, she used to say. Vivian McCune opened the front door and waved us in. She was an attractive woman with an infectious laugh.

"Betha," she said and hugged Ma hello. "It's been too long. I'm so glad to see you. You haven't gotten a day older. My gracious, what in the world have you brought?"

Ma handed her the basket of fried pies.

"Betha," she drawled, and Ma's name seemed longer when she said it. "You shouldn't have brought all these fried pies. They do smell wonderful. Are they your pineapple ones?"

Ma nodded and smiled.

"We'll be fat as pigs," Vivian said, laughing. "JL still talks about your pineapple pies."

"Oh, for heaven's sake," Ma said. But you could tell the compliments pleased her. "Vivian, we're so glad to have you all back. George and I have really missed you and JL. It can get pretty dull around here when the fun people are gone."

"We're glad to be back, I can tell you. JL hadn't been working in a while." She paused and looked at me. "Well, now, what else did you bring with you besides these pies?"

"This is Glenn's daughter, Sheila Rae," Ma said. "Glenn and Selma and Sheila Rae live with Selma's mother, Louise, right up the street from you. She's going into the second grade. She was so excited to know she'll have some other girls to play with in the neighborhood."

I tried to look hopeful. "Where are your girls?" I asked.

"You wait right here. They're in their room playing," she said. "Tinabeth, Sarah Katherine. Come out here," she called towards the back of the house. "You've got company."

At this moment a chunky little girl with brown curly hair came running into the living room dragging a red wagon with a doll sitting in it. All of a sudden everything got noisy. Wagon wheels rolling on the linoleum floor and then screeching to a halt. She pulled up short and stared at me.

"Sarah Katherine, this is Sheila Rae," Vivian said to her younger daughter. "Where's your sister?"

"Right here," someone said. I turned to look as the other sister came strolling in. I think I stopped breathing. I know I stared. Before me stood the prettiest girl I had ever seen in my life. Her hazel eyes were perfectly set in a face that was as smooth as silk. Her brunette curls hung loosely and seemed to move in different directions all at once. But what I couldn't believe were her lips. They were incredible.

It would be years before I heard the terms pouty or petulant or sultry or probably even sexy. But from that moment on, I knew that lips must be what held the secrets of the universe and that these lips would be the standard by which all others would be measured. I was smitten.

Ma, ever attuned to something not quite right, said nervously, "Sheila Rae, say hello to Tinabeth and Sarah Katherine. Where in the world are your manners?"

I couldn't say a word. I felt like I wasn't even there really. This was a stranger pretending to be me. This person was mute. I watched helplessly as Sarah Katherine and Tinabeth pulled the wagon to the door to go outside.

"Come on," Sarah Katherine said loudly as the wagon clattered against the screen door. I fell into step behind the wagon. I would be forever grateful to her.

Brian Breitenstein

Breaking the Barbie Habit

"IS THIS A MEAL FOR A BOY OR A GIRL?"

I still remember being a child, probably around the age of six or seven, and going to McDonald's with my mom. I naturally got the cheeseburger Happy Meal, plain of course. And then the drive-thru attendant would ask that question. I always shuddered. I knew that if my mom said "boy" a mini version of a yellow Tonka truck would be buried beneath my french fries in the Happy Meal box. After much hesitation, I answered my mom, she answered the attendant, and we were told to pull up to the first window.

I didn't have any siblings growing up. I was an only child on my mom's side and I was way younger than all the other kids on my dad's side. We didn't live in a neighborhood, so I had no friends nearby. The only relative I had that was remotely close to me in age was my cousin Stacy, who was still six years my senior. She was, regardless of our age difference, my favorite relative. We spent all of our time together. She must have been about eleven years old when she introduced me to her favorite toy: Barbie. What girl didn't grow up with Barbie dolls and Barbie houses and Barbie convertibles? What boy didn't? Well, probably most of them, or at least the ones whose best friends weren't an eleven-year-old female cousin. I didn't fall into that category. Barbie became quite a constant in my life at that age. My parents were actually quite accepting of this. Even more surprisingly, when it came time to rid me of my Barbie habit, it was my mother, a lesbian, who made the first move. To this day, I don't quite understand that. My father, a straight male, continued buying me Barbie dolls for a few years after my mom prohibited them. I didn't let this bother me. Or stop me.

So we would pull up to the window, pay the drive-thru worker, take our food, and head off for home. I'd open my Happy Meal and smile when my eyes fell upon the miniature Disney Barbie. Yes, I was a boy. Yes, I had, not five minutes ago, asked for a toy for a girl. What did that mean? Why did I have to make a choice like that? Why didn't they just ask if the child preferred to have a Tonka truck or a doll? This was probably one of the first major encounters I experienced dealing with gender roles in society. For a six-year-old boy to have to tell his mother he wants the "toy for a girl" is extremely difficult, if not embarrassing. Embarrassed as I was, I continued this habit for several years until I finally broke myself of my own Barbie habit.

What was my mom trying to tell me by outlawing Barbie in our house? Why, in the eyes of the corporate America, was I a little girl? Can a boy not play with a Disney Barbie just as easily? These were all questions I struggled with while growing up. Some of those issues still travel with me today. Ultimately, I'm sure these issues have a strong correlation with the struggle and realization I had with my sexuality while growing up. I was being taught that one toy was meant to be played with only by little girls. Did ordering that girl Happy Meal make me less of a boy? Of course not.

To be honest, whenever I go to McDonald's now, I still tell the drive-thru attendant to give me the Happy Meal with the Barbie in it.

Ed Madden

Becoming a Man

WHEN I WAS IN JUNIOR HIGH in the mid-1970s, two of my friends, Dudley and Charles, pulled me aside in Coach Simmons's history class and told me to stop carrying my books "like a girl." I was in seventh grade. I played the clarinet. I had zits and glasses and braces. I had spontaneous erections during English class and clumsy feet in gym. I had a body that seemed determined to embarrass me. And I carried my books in my arms as if I were holding a baby, carried them, that is, "like a girl." I carried a lot of books—I was a rather nerdy kid—and since I carried so many, it seemed natural to hold my books the way I did. But I quickly learned that guys—if they carry books at all—carry their books in one hand, slung loosely against a hip. Though I would never excel in sports or take shop or agriculture classes or brag about my heterosexual exploits—things I saw my male friends doing—I did learn to carry my books like a guy.

About the same time that Dudley and Charles told me to stop carrying my books like a girl, I was also trying out for the junior high basketball team, mostly to please my father. I wasn't interested in sports of any kind, but I was interested in trying out for basketball since my father had been a basketball star in high school. I wanted to be in his shoes—literally. I even played in his old Chuck Taylor's. But my father's shoes were a little too tight, too confining. And the ingrown toenail I developed just confirmed for me my failure to fill his shoes and to make the team. Looking back at yearbook pictures from that era, I can say now, yes, I was a sissy—though for years I would have resented that word. But there were those Elton John glasses in junior high school. The Barry Manilow—or was it Shaun Cassidy—hair of my senior year. And that totally femmy bellbottom drum major uniform, with the satin-lined inverted pleats at the cuff of those flared legs and a big white hat draped with a dazzlingly large orange plume.

I was also beginning to realize during those junior high years something of my sexuality, the desires I would do my best to repress and deny and misunderstand for several years. I was told at church camp that I threw "like a girl"—and I was always put way out in outfield during church camp softball so that I would have as little contact with the ball as possible. When I was told that I carried my books "like a girl," or threw a ball "like a girl," or swung a bat "like a girl," I knew what was being said. For to carry my books "like a girl," to walk "like a girl," to throw a baseball "like a girl" could mean, at least unconsciously, that I would also like "like a girl"—that I would not like girls, but, like a girl, I would like men. So when two friends told me to stop carrying my books "like a girl," it was a moment charged with possible meanings about not only what kind of boy I was, but also what kind of man I might become. My incomplete gender performance was just a symptom of my potential for further failures in masculinity.

Sissies are a problem for both the anti-gay and the gay movement. In anti-gay literature, "feminine" behaviors and interests are flagged as indicators of possible homosexuality, and anti-gay therapists set their sights on "sissy" boys because they insist correcting seemingly "feminine" behavior is an early intervention into the lives of "pre-homosexual" boys. Sissies, though, are a problem for many gay men as well, and we suffer from what one writer calls our own "effeminophobia." "No fems" say the personal ads, and the biggest argument before the first South Carolina Pride festival was over the participation of drag queens.

In our attempts to butch up our past selves, to make that powerful asser-
tion that men as men can desire other men, we too often feel a need
to de-emphasize the links between homosexuality and gender performance—and between gay adults and children who refuse to conform to
gender norms, that is, between our adult selves and our own histories
as tomboys and sissies.

Not all of us were sissies. I know that. But all of us grow up in a
culture that links gender and sexual identity. Becoming a man isn't the
result, necessarily, of genitals, chromosomes, or hormones—though
testosterone and chromosomes play their part. We learn to become men
through the conscious and unconscious expectations of those around
us, as well as through the social and cultural gender norms we learn
from childhood. Though Dudley and Charles would never have used
words like "gender norms," they were deadly earnest—the way junior
high boys can be—asking me to carry my books differently. They didn't
want to hang out with a sissy.

By the time we got to high school, we'd grown apart as friends.
Band and football are difficult worlds to bridge. I never had sex in high
school, but I learned a lot about sex in high school. I grew up in a small
town in the rural South during the 1970s, a world of evangelical religion, economic depression, and religious devotion to high school football. Anyone from the South can tell you about the importance of high
school football, and my hometown was no different. A winning team
gets all kinds of perks from the local booster club, including team trips
to bowl games. One year the team went to Memphis for the Liberty Bowl.
During that trip, a rich boy hired a prostitute for the team to share. They
took turns with her in a hotel room. I'm not sure how common such
heterosexual male bonding is, though inevitably one hears of similar
stories. Another team trip was to the Sugar Bowl in New Orleans. While
there, the boys quickly hit the local porn theaters. One boy—the hero
of the story as it was told and retold in the halls of my high school—was
propositioned at a theater by another man. Outraged, the boy started a
fight, and, as the story went, he picked up the "faggot" and threw him
through a window at the back of the theater. His teammates told this
story of homosexual panic with approval and awe.

I learned about the kind of man I might become—and the kind of man I didn't want to be—from those stories of adolescent male bonding, stories built around objectified women and assaults on gay men. With Magnum P.I. on television and the Village People on the radio, masculinity was becoming interesting to me, in stranger and stranger ways. But I also gleaned something of other gender possibilities from the New Wave magazines my friend Elizabeth loaned me in senior English—all those punks and glam rockers and queer Brits.

We like to think that sexual and gender identity come to us naturally. Indeed, more often than not we assume that biological sex and socialized gender—as well as the complicated mix of nature and nurture we call "sexuality"—are normally and naturally connected. However, becoming "a man," whatever that may mean, may be anything but natural—as those of us who liked Barbie dolls, Easy Bake ovens, and macramé projects are all too aware. And as any drag king can tell you.

Sometimes becoming a man just means learning how to act like one.

Sheila Gets a Shave

"GEORGE, HERE COMES SHEILA for her shave," said Old Man Tom Grissom, who was already in his favorite spot in the barbershop by the time I got there.

Ma, my grandmother, who had been married to Barber George Morris for over forty years, said Tom Grissom ought to pay rent for all the time he spent sitting on that bench in the shop. Pa, my grandfather the barber, just laughed like he always did. He'd be charging rent to a lot of old men if he ever got started on that. The barbershop was a thriving business on Main Street in Richards, Texas. Main Street was the only paved street in Richards (Population 440), and Pa was the sole barber in the area. People drove from all over Grimes County to his out-of-the-way shop with one barber's chair, bought in the 1930s when he first opened. Waiting patrons and gossipy old men sat on two wooden benches.

Past the benches was a shoeshine stand that Pa used when somebody wanted shiny boots. Along the wall behind the barber's chair were a long mirror and two shelves that held the glass display boxes. One of the boxes housed the gleaming scissors, combs, and brushes for hair-cuts. The other held shaving mugs, razors, and Old Spice bottles for the shaves. Everything was spotless.

Pa was happy to see me.

"Hey, sugar. You here for your shave?" he asked.

"I sure am, Barber Morris," I replied in my most grown-up customer voice. It was the summer after my first grade in school, and I loved to come to the barbershop. Sometimes I brought my knife and sat on the porch outside the shop and whittled with the old men who lolled there for hours just talking and whittling. Other times, I had business with my grandfather. Like today.

Pa got out the little booster seat and put it in the barber's chair so I could climb up on it. I was too small to sit in the chair without it.

"How about a haircut with your shave? That pretty blonde hair is getting too long for this summer heat," he said.

"No, thanks, Pa. Mama always tells me when to get my hair cut," I said. "Just a shave today." Old Man Tom Grissom nodded at this.

"I sure wouldn't be cutting that blonde hair without Selma knowing," he said. "She's mighty particular about things."

"I appreciate your advice, Tom," Pa said with a trace of annoyance. "But Sheila Rae and I are just having a conversation for fun. Nothing serious."

Meantime, Pa had placed the thin white sheet over me and leaned the chair back just far enough to start to work. He lathered up the shaving cream in his mug with the brush and dabbed it on my face. I loved the smell of the shaving cream. He let that soak while he took the razor strop and swished it up and down slowly and methodically to get it just right. It didn't matter to me that he was using the side without the blade. It made the same swishing noise.

Then, he took the bladeless side of the razor and gave me the best shave ever. He was very careful to get every part of my face. He even pinched my nose so that he got the part between my mouth and nose just so. Pa was an artist with his razor and scissors.

He put a warm, wet, white-cotton, laundered towel over my face and rubbed off the last of the shaving cream. It felt so clean. Finally, he took the Old Spice After Shave and gave it a good shake, rubbed it on his hands, and then on my face and neck. Nothing beats the aroma of Old Spice.

Old Man Tom Grissom said, "Well, that ought to do you for a week or so, won't it?"

"Yes," I said. "Probably so. We'll see."

Pa gave me the worn yellow hand mirror that he gave to all of his customers to inspect his handiwork. I studied my face thoughtfully.

"Well, how does it look to you?" he asked with a smile and nodded with satisfaction. "Time to pay up. That'll be two bits for the shave. That's with the favorite-granddaughter discount."

"Very good, Barber Morris. Much obliged." I reached into my jeans pocket and brought out some play money coins and handed them to Pa. Just about that time, Ma drove up and got out of her car.

"George, what's Sheila Rae doing in that chair?" she bristled.

Old Man Tom Grissom said, "Betha, Sheila Rae's here for her shave."

Ma gave him a withering look. I got down from the barber's chair and ran over to Ma and tried to reassure her that everything was all right. Ma looked at Pa and said this was just what she had been telling him the other night about encouraging me in all of this foolishness.

"She shouldn't be spending her summer hanging around this shop," she said, looking accusingly at Pa, who said nothing.

"Ma, can I have a nickel to go get an ice cream cone at the drug store? Getting a shave makes me hungry." Ma never said no to me, so I got my nickel and left. I walked across the street to Mr. McAfee's drug store and got my Blue Bell vanilla cone and headed home.

I saw Ma and Pa still in animated conversation at the shop.

Old Man Tom Grissom had gone home.

David R. Gillespie

At the Corner of Sex and Dixie

I DON'T KNOW WHAT IT WAS that made me pick up James Sears's book *Growing Up Gay in the South*. It might have been the title. But I'm more inclined to think it was the juxtaposition of the word "gay" with that Confederate battle flag on the cover. They seemed, at first glance, to be incongruous. Gay? The South? The fact of the matter is, I am as irrevocably Southern as I am irreversibly queer. Nature and nurture.

I'm convinced that there must be a genetic component to my being queer. Don't think there is any getting around that. It's not all that's involved in the determination of my being attracted to members of the same gender, but it is a part. And I couldn't help being a Southerner. I was raised by adoptive parents whose families had deep and distinct roots in the South. Way back to the 1700s.

I am queer. I am Southern. I wholeheartedly embrace both.

My friends, especially those from other regions of the country, sometimes look at me weirdly when I profess my love of the South. They just don't get it. After all, isn't the South supposed to be the buckle of the Bible Belt? Actually, the Midwest is, but I let them believe what they will. True, religion, specifically Christianity, is an integral part of the warp and woof of the South. It is, as Flannery O'Connor so aptly dubbed it, the Christ-haunted landscape. But that's okay. Just as I've come to realize that there in nothing intrinsically contradictory about being both queer and religious, I've also realized that it's quite possible, if not downright enjoyable, to be Southern and queer.

In fact, in my more zealous moments, I like to argue that being Southern and queer and a writer kinda places me in a distinguished line of such folks: queer Southern storytellers. There is, to be a little biblical, a great host of witnesses whose writings and lives have brilliantly demonstrated the intersection of sex and Dixie.

Growing up queer in the South of the 1960s and 1970s was something for which I will be eternally grateful. It was a culture of contrasts, of huntin' and fishin' good ol' boys against the refined (dare I say "queer") approach to life found in Leslie Howard's portrayal of Ashley Wilkes in GWTW (that's *Gone With The Wind*, for you non-Southerners).

I had aunts and uncles who were most likely queer, but they were never called such. They were "old maids" and "bachelors." I had cousins who were described to me as "queer" by my mother, not in the sexual sense of that word, but simply as different. You know, cultured, refined. Two of them have since come out to me.

At T.L. Hanna High School in Anderson, we had womanless beauty pageants. Can I call them drag shows? Most often the most beautiful "women" were the football players. Those guys who were "sensitive" or "refined" were probably afraid to be in the pageant less it hit just a little too close to home.

I can also honestly say I never heard a sermon during my Southern childhood about the sin of homosexuality. And, thanks to my good Presbyterian parents, I was in church every time the door was opened. When I had my first boyfriend at the ripe old age of thirteen, I thought it was perfectly normal. Though I have to confess, I did get caught fooling around with a guy by my father once. He really didn't say anything, other than it was nasty, and told me not to dare do it again—but then, he didn't say much about anything.

I love being queer. I also love being a Southerner. I love the South— with all of its warts.

One particular reason I love it so is that we are a storytelling people. Before television, much less the Internet, had come to dominate our lives, we told stories. I have vivid memories of sitting around my great Aunt Jessie's dining room table, listening to various family members recount tales from the past and present. Both were of value to us.

Young queer boys and girls growing up in today's South face some different challenges. A militant, theocratic evangelical type of Christianity has taken over many of the churches. With the advent and development of "gay rights" struggles have come the inevitable backlash from the pulpit. We have been for a while the sin du jour, having replaced racial matters, communism, and other "liberal" issues. These queer youth need to hear our stories and they need to develop their own. And we older folks, those of previous generations of story-makers and tellers, we need to listen to theirs.

Above all, in my opinion, we need to somehow enable them to see that being queer is absolutely nothing to be ashamed of—and neither is being Southern—that living at the intersection of sex and Dixie is not only quite possible, it can be quite fulfilling as well.

Connor Gillis

Don't They Know That's Dangerous?

NEW YORK CITY. Where the sun sets early and Greenwich Village is a legend. I had never been before. I chose visiting my cousin Jess as a good excuse for both. It was there, in the heart of NYC, that I was reminded of how used to oppression I have become. Maybe my comfort with hate is why I am cynical and often bitter. Maybe not.

Jess and I were strolling down Seventh or Eighth Avenue, or some other numbered avenue in Manhattan, when a pair of men stepped in front of us, trying to avoid being run over by a soccer mom and her destructive stroller. With a glance one could tell they were gay—well-dressed, Prada sunglasses (wearing them in the dark, no less), well-fitting slacks, and brightly-colored collared shirts. I hate to promote stereotypes, but, honestly, anyone with a glimmer of gaydar would be able to pick these two up on their radar. As I gave them the obvious "Family!" look, I noticed they were holding hands. In public. At night. In a city. Surrounded by strangers.

"Don't they know that's dangerous?" I whispered.

"What?" my cousin asked.

"Holding hands like that in public."

I was answered with a look that clearly suggested that this was the norm. Later, I explained to her why I was so shocked. I'm from a very rural, very Southern Baptist Georgia town of barely seven thousand. It's one of those places where everyone knows you by your first name and the sight of your car. I was the first "out" gay, lesbian, transsexual, queer, or anything-other-than-straight student in the high school. Teachers didn't know what to do with me. My friends, who were also gay, were outed simply by being associated with me. It was chaos, chaos that all happened because I fell in love with a girl.

It was obvious; we were never apart. She swept me up and took me away. I even forgot my name the first time we were introduced. Meredith was hers. People suspected, and I got careless and tired of sneaking around, so I came out. The end. Actually, that was only the beginning. A wave of violence started. My high school was the kind of place that made private Catholic schools look slack. Each year they tried to enforce uniforms. Each year they put a plethora of restrictions upon us. And each year the student body got more and more rebellious. However, the mindset of the principal, many of the teachers, and the board of education was like a sealed box. When it came to homosexuality, they told us that we were going to hell, that we deserved the hate we got.

Every day my friends were beaten up—the more flamboyant gay boys got the worst of it. I was heckled in classrooms and quickly learned that the safest place to sit was in the corner so that two of my sides were protected by cinder block walls. Teachers turned a blind eye to the taunts and beatings, and also a deaf ear to the repeated taunts of "faggot!" and "dyke!" that we got in every classroom.

Thankfully, my friends and I were all honors kids, and we all conveniently met Ms. Worsham at some point in our high school careers. Her devil's-advocate attitude in debates on topics such as gay marriage (before it was a big to-do with the media), abortion, Bush, and various other things tipped us off that she was far more socially liberal than any other official in the school. She became our safe haven. All eight of us would lie low in her classroom for nearly forty-five minutes after the last bell each day before we'd dare venture in the parking lot. Bill's broken arm taught us that. After waiting, we'd all go to our cars together. We parked next to each other since we got to school before the teachers arrived, taking refuge in the hallways. And each day one of our cars would be damaged. Mine got the worst. All four tires slashed over five times a year, windows broken at least four times a quarter, tail lights and head lights broken nearly every week, and a new hate-word keyed into my paint every day. By the time I graduated, my '91 Volvo was hate-crime art on wheels.

It gets worse. We all didn't make it out of high school. Two murdered, three suicides. All hate-crime related and all treated as "depression meds gone wrong" or "freak accidents." I'm used to watching my back, used to the hard life of being out, used to being confronted with violence on a daily basis. Every day it amazes me how different and how accepting the industrial areas of the North can be. Sadly, I don't think I'll ever be trusting enough to hold hands with my girlfriend like those boys on the street in NYC.

Ashleigh Witt

Prom 2002

PROM. 2002. I am a junior in high school and have only recently returned to my alma mater. Yellow jackets. The junior board is busy preparing for Mardi Gras. I am not shocked by how few of my classmates know where Mardi Gras is held. Plastic beads. I don't have a date yet. A girl who lives on my street tries to get me to go with her friend. "He is in band," she says. As if that is all the information I might need to make a decision.

Drummer. He bails out at the last minute. Dating some new girl. She would be jealous. I only met him once. At a Huddle House, in Sumter. I complain to my drama class that I don't have a date. The next day a girl tells me a kid from class wants to ask me to go. Nice.

The kid from class is named Cory. Blonde-haired, blue-eyed, and a fairly decent actor by most standards. Mostly his. Pre-prom includes pictures in the park. Finlay. And then dinner at some nice restaurant downtown. I am surprised when he pays. We are not a couple. Friends. The limo rides through downtown. An undercover cop sits with the driver trying to catch us drinking. Underage. Boys grabbing their girlfriends' chests and girls pretending they are annoyed. Not mine.

The dance hall is garishly decorated with masks and the sort. Purple

and yellow, green and gold. Couples take standard prom portraits—
some are bad, some are decent. Most are horrid. Not us. Cory dances
with everyone. I dance, too. Electric slide. We are together for the slow
dances. We laugh at the other couples. Girls with their heads on boys'
shoulders. So silly. "I heard she is pregnant," he says. Not surprised. We
move together across the floor and sit through the next few songs. "Big
party after the prom at Casey's house. Her parents will let us drink if
we promise not to leave," Cory says. Pinky swear. I think the punch is
spiked. Already a little tipsy. I wish they served food. The school is too
cheap. Not even hors d'oeuvres. Cheap!

A club song comes on. I decide to get up. We move to the middle of
the floor. Dance.

Dance. Smile and hold hands. Laugh at the other students. Laugh at
the so-called prom queen. Student body president all in white. Talia. She
was nice. The crowd is getting bigger. More and more students on the
floor. More and more students in the building. They don't have tickets.
No one checks.

A group in a corner. There is a boy dancing with another boy. I know
his face, but not his name. They are both dressed in black suits. Handsome. They move together as well. On the same beat. In front of each
other. They are looking into each other's eyes. Staring. More people are
gathering around. The music is getting louder. A crescendo. The two do
not seem to notice. Lost. They are alone, alone in a crowded room. Alone
in their own world. Neither pays attention to the increasing hostility.

More and more people now. Teachers. Administrators. Cops. There
is a barricade between the boys and the rest of the prom. A wall. No
one in and no one out. You can't move. Barely breathe. Chants. Taunts.
Snide remarks spit like venom. "Fags." "Queers." Barely audible over my
beating heart. My ears are red hot. Share awkward glances with Cory. Do
we stay or do we go? "Break it up!" The cops move towards the couple. A
couple. They are a couple. Not like me and Cory. Just friends. They are a
couple. A real couple. I don't know many real couples. Parents. Maybe.

The music stops. The crowd clears. The cops leave. The teachers leave.
The boys leave. Couple.

I run after Cory. Outside in the parking lot next to a red car. Sitting on the curb he stares at the stars. Warm night. I put my hand on his shoulder. He doesn't look up. "I'm sorry," I say. Nothing. We watch the others walk to their cars and rentals. A sea of pastels and taffeta. Ugly, for the most part. Rented tuxes. Cory owns his. Laughter. People are joking. Yelling and screaming. Chiding each other. Cory looks up at me. His eyes are moist. A smile. "It will never stop," he says.

I take his hand. I know it hasn't even begun for Cory. No one knows. Prom 2002.

Ed Madden

Smear the Queer:
A Lesson from the Playground

WHEN MARK NICHOLSON SPILLED his milk on me in the school cafeteria in first grade, my teacher, Mrs. Jackson, filled my glass and let me pour it on his head. It was a strange way to teach good behavior and a strange way to deal with bullies, but that's what we did in 1969 in rural Arkansas. That was the year that I played a wise man in the school Christmas play, in a blue bathrobe and cotton-ball beard. The year that Carroll Toddy fell backwards out of the seat of a swing. It knocked him out and left an enormous knot on his round head. It was an image we all remembered for the rest of our three years at Rutherford Elementary School—and a cautionary tale whenever we sought to soar too high.

For three years, before we were bused off to Newport to join the city kids, all of us country kids spent our time together at Rutherford Elementary, a little country school with maybe twenty students per grade, three teachers, and a big playground, site of my most vivid memories. There was an old seesaw bar—seesaws gone—which we called the tightrope as we teetered down it, sometimes holding a teacher's hand, sometimes alone. The big rock near the sand bed, inevitable site of King of the

Hill, until a teacher saw us and forced us to stop, as they sometimes did when our games got too rough or someone ran to them in tears. And a big yard on the west side of the school, where we played football and softball and chase and Red Rover.

On cold days, the teams devolved into a game of Kill the Man with the Ball, more often than not called Smear the Queer, a phrase we shouted as we played. A boy with a ball would run the field, the rest of us after him, trying to tag or tackle him. Tagged or tackled, he might toss the ball, lob it into the mob of us, or hurl it high. Snag it, and you're it. In possession of the ball, you were the queer. And as the rest of the name suggests, it was the goal of everyone else to "smear" you—"smear" a loose term that became looser as the game progressed—"smear" meaning tackle, meaning grab or trip, meaning kick, meaning punch. No out of bounds, no teams, and no rules beyond the simple and repeated shout of "smear the queer, smear the queer." And so it went until a bell called us back inside for school.

There was no way to win.

In March of 2007, Democratic State Representative Seth Whipper of Charleston introduced a bill that makes it a felony to assault or harass someone on the basis of his or her race, religion, age, ethnic background, sexual orientation, or gender identity. A similar bill was proposed in the Senate by Democratic Senator Robert Ford, also of Charleston.

South Carolina is one of four states in the nation with no hate-crimes law—along with Indiana, Arkansas (where I learned to play Smear the Queer), and Wyoming (home of Matthew Shepard, who died in October 1998 as the result of a brutal anti-gay beating).

A hate-crimes bill was also under consideration at the national level, though our own local representative, Republican Joe Wilson—ever dependable as a parrot of right-wing talking points—wrote to constituents in May that he voted against it because the inclusion of sexual orientation would, he argued, "inhibit the free practice of religion." If the law passed, preachers could say what they want in the pulpit, but unless they expect their parishioners to go out the front door of the church and punch gay folks—that is, unless Wilson considered the physical assault and harassment of others a form of sound Christian doctrine—I don't see how this legislation inhibits religious practice.

Hate-crimes laws have been introduced before in the South Carolina legislature, but they've never passed. In 1999, the South Carolina Senate passed a hate-crimes bill, but the state House, controlled by anti-gay legislators, failed to pass it *because* it included sexual orientation. A hate-crimes bill had been suggested in 1997, after the burning of several African-American churches. By 1998, the murder of Matthew Shepard confirmed, at least for some, that sexual orientation should be included in hate crimes legislation. According to *The State* newspaper, Charlie Condon, the attorney general at the time, refused to support the bill. In March of 1997, he dismissively stated that feminists and gay-rights activists had hijacked the bill "to bring attention to their various grievances against society." Republican leaders followed Condon's lead and killed the bill in the House because it included gays and lesbians. As hate crimes laws come under consideration again, the murder of Sean Kennedy outside a bar in Greenville has added force to the inclusion of sexual orientation.

Though I left Smear the Queer on the grounds of Rutherford Elementary, the lesson stuck. In later years, I would realize that Smear the Queer takes many forms, social and political, as well as physical. All those sentimental homilies tell us that everything you need to know in life, you learn in the first years of school. It's true. Don't swing too high. Watch out for bullies. If you get picked last, you're a sissy. Tag, you're it. And smear the queer.

When I played Smear the Queer as a kid, I don't recall ever grabbing the ball myself. Only boys who were quick or tough did so, the ones able to evade others in the chase, or those ready simply to shove off any attempted tackle. Of course, we didn't know what queers were back then. We just knew that you were supposed to smear them.

Unfortunately, it's an all-too common and lasting lesson.

On May 6, 2007, Sean Kennedy was punched outside a Greenville bar by a young man calling him a "faggot." The punch broke all of his facial bones, and the fall on the asphalt separated his brain from his brain stem. He later died from the injuries. His attacker was charged with involuntary manslaughter, receiving a five-year sentence that was later suspended to three. He was released in 2009 after serving only a year. Kennedy's mother, Elke Kennedy, founded the organization Sean's Last Wish to raise awareness about hate crimes.

On October 28, 2009, President Barack Obama signed the Matthew Shepard and James Byrd, Jr. Hate Crimes Prevention Act into law—a federal hate crimes law that includes sexual orientation.

Trixie Trash

Bullies

I WAS THE CLASS SISSY from day one. Singe factor of one-twenty. You know the type. The kid who would rather jump rope with the girls than play football with the boys. Jacks instead of toy soldiers. Hopscotch instead of tag. Or the kid who sits by himself, away from the others, because he has no "real friends" and "no one wants to play with him." The loner. I was also a crybaby. However, I only cried when people hit me or were mean to me.

I cried a lot.

Maybe that's why I had no friends. I just didn't see the vicious circle. As the years passed, classmates broke into their separate groups— the jocks, the cheerleaders, the brains, the heads, the Future Farmers of America, the bad kids who smoked cigarettes in the smoking shed during recess.

And the little gay boy. I was a group unto myself. I became easy to bully because I never fought back. I just ran away. I never changed. I just ran away. I ran away from the confrontations. I ran away from the pain. I ran away into my imagination. It was safe there.

At home, my father was an evil bully of a man. Years later, after high school, my mother told me he had been a member of the Klan. And that explained a lot. When I was eight and my little brother, James, was four, my father would go to the butcher and get a fresh box of cow bones and sockets with some meat on them. He would take it and us next door to our grandmother's house to feed her snarly, snappy hunting dogs. It would be late at night in an area that, to this day, I still believe to be haunted.

And he would leave us.

Now, it was just next door, maybe seventy yards. No real danger. But he would leave us. And we would be frozen with fear. And when we finally broke free and ran for our house, he would be hiding behind a tree. He would jump out, yell, and chase us back to the house.

I guess that's when I started to develop "trust issues."

I hated that man. When I was around six, I remember my father pulling out his pocketknife and saying to me, "You want to be a girl so bad, come here! I'm gonna cut your tally whacker off!"

The joke, though, was on him. I said, "Okay."

He died when I was eleven.

"Oh, Trixie! You have unresolved father-anger issues."

"*Ya think?*"

One day, after gym class, two classmates, Alan and Frank, were following me. They were teasing me and calling me names. As usual, I just ignored them and kept walking. As usual. Another classmate, Tommy, a rather big jock who sometimes picked on me, too, was walking ahead of me. He turned around and came back to Alan and Frank, and he yelled at them. "Don't pick on him! If you want to pick on someone, pick on me! Yeah. I didn't think so."

Tommy turned to me and barked, "Come on!" And we walked away.

It's very strange when one of your bullies comes to rescue you from your other bullies. I was so shocked that I didn't even ask him why he had done that. Nor did I thank him. A few weeks later, I was sitting behind this hero-bully in class. It was the end of the day and the teacher, Ms. Morris, was out of the room. I tapped Tommy on the shoulder to ask a question. He turned around, grabbed me by the throat, and choked me. Hard.

And then, he turned back without saying a word. The other students just giggled and laughed. And when the teacher returned, no one said a thing. Not even me.

I had an after school job in the next town. I washed dishes in a pizza restaurant. I loved that job because there were no bullies. The cook was a college student named Reggie. I loved Reggie like a big brother. He was upbeat. He was high-energy. And, his friendship helped me build my self-esteem. He could always make me laugh. But not that night. The choking had sent me into a state of silence, and the humiliation in class had filled me with shame. Near the end of the night, Reggie called his girlfriend, Gina, and she stopped by.

I liked Gina, too. We had things in common. We both tap-danced and we both loved her boyfriend. She pulled me aside to find out what was wrong. The two of them made me talk, and the cry baby returned.

You know those cries. The kind where you can't catch your breath and you are about to hyperventilate? The kind when your heart breaks and you cry so hard that snot comes out of your nose? One of those cries. They tried their best, but it's hard to comfort an inconsolable sixteen-year-old that has turned into a puddle of mucous and tears.

After high school, I went to Francis Marion College. Because I liked the name. And they accepted my test scores. It was 1980, and Francis Marion had built on-campus apartments. I was lucky enough to get a room. I would have three roommates, each with his own room. We would share a kitchen, a bathroom, and a living room.

A few weeks before I was to leave for college, I was at the gay bar, McB's. The drinking age was eighteen, and I was feeling nervous about college, so I had a few drinks. Okay, a bottle and a half of champagne. I was sloppy drunk and in drag, *and*, even at eighteen, it was not a pretty sight. I confessed to my friend, Sally, about how nervous I was about the future roommates and being gay and what should I do? She said not to worry. Go to college, tell your roommates you are gay—first thing—and everything will be fine.

She then dumped me in my car and asked some other drag queens to drive me home. They did, and promptly stole my car until the next day. Bitches.

So, I arrived at college and after meeting my roommates, we went to McDonald's. I told them everything—that I was gay, *and* a drag queen, *and* my name was "Trixie." They took it very well. They didn't beat me up. They looked kind of confused, and they didn't say much, but that was alright because I was the one doing all the talking. Everything seemed fine.

A few days later, I was returning to the apartment. It was nighttime, and I was carrying a big box of clothes. I walked past the next-door apartment. The windows were open and I heard someone say, "There he is! There's that faggot! QUEER! QUEER! QUEER!"

I fumbled with the keys, trying to get the door open. Five big guys came out of that apartment. They walked over and stood around me and smacked their fists against their hands. (Meaty, smacking sounds.) I got inside and locked the door. They just stood outside and called me a few more names. In the kitchen, I found a note from another apartment inviting us to a "Welcome to College Party." The P.S. said, "Don't bring Trixie."

The next day, one of the roommates said that he had asked for a transfer to another apartment because he "couldn't live with a gay guy." The other two didn't want me there either. So, once again, I ran away.

You might think that, sooner or later, bullying stops. You would be wrong. It just takes different forms: the anti-gay politicians who demonize us, and the social forces that continue to isolate and shame us. The "religious right" is wrong, but that doesn't stop them from bullying us.

I'm tired of running.

The only thing left to do is stand and fight.

Nick Slaughter

From Phobe to Friend

I HAD NOT MET CAM BEFORE move-in day at the university, but on that day I made the unconscious assumption that he was straight. Nothing about him suggested anything else to me; he wasn't the flamboyant fairy that I, at the time, would have expected of a gay man. I wouldn't have thought there was anything "different" about him until a new mutual acquaintance told me that she thought he was gay only because he held his cigarette like a girl. The seed of that old irrational fear had been planted. For a few weeks, I began amassing more and more trivial evidence in my mind until one evening I sat alone in our dorm room and decided to answer the question: could I live with a gay man? My exposure to gay people had been limited, to say the least, and nothing in my experience had left me prepared to live with a gay roommate.

The earliest memory I could recall of a substantial encounter with a gay person was in the sixth grade, nearly nine years ago. We attended the same middle school, and we were in the same grade. His name was Stewart, and the first time I learned anything about him, of course, was from second-hand gossip. One day, a girl told a story about this boy Stewart who had gone to the doctor's office where her mother worked as a nurse. The mother had made small talk with Stewart, capitalizing on the topic that she thought was universal for all young boys: she asked Stewart if he liked any girls at his school. In the story, Stewart promptly laughed out loud at the nurse as if she were a fool. Upon hearing this story, I was immediately uncomfortable. In fact, I developed a very irrational fear of this boy even though I never had a class with Stewart in all three of my years at the school. Any time I passed him in the hall, that same fear would seize me, as if his very presence was a threatening force. I would think of him as the "gay kid," never accepting that there existed any other aspect of his being. Fortunately, I never progressed beyond fear to hate, only tormenting myself rather than those around me, like Stewart.

Stewart was the only person in my primary school career who I would personally identify as gay, never noticing the differences of others that must have been around me. Of course I had, and probably still do have, a heterocentrism that blinded me to the fact that some guys were attracted to other guys and some girls were attracted to other girls.

During the last semester of my senior year in high school, I was taking the required class on American government. The most interesting moments in the class were the individual conversations I would have with the teacher. We spoke after one class about the issue of gay marriage. I cited the passage in the Declaration of Independence: "All men are created equal, [and] they are endowed by their Creator with certain unalienable Rights, that among these are Life, Liberty and the pursuit of Happiness." Though the Declaration is not law, our country is said to operate upon these principles, so I said to my teacher that I didn't understand how the government couldn't recognize gay marriages. The government was immorally and hypocritically denying homosexuals their "happiness." My teacher reflected that, in its history, America hasn't usually lived up to the principles of the Declaration. My abstract support of gay marriage, however, didn't change my irrational fear of gay people.

In my first year of college, I sat and considered the fate of my friendship with my possibly-gay roommate. Some time passed as I thought alone until I finally came to a conclusion: what does it matter whether my roommate is straight or gay? *Nothing at all.* So he's gay. What does that really change about him? He was still the person I had been living with for two months. And what if he were to bring another guy back to the room with him? It wouldn't make a difference if Cam was gay or straight. I wouldn't want to be in the room if he were having sex, no matter who the other person was.

This rational conclusion was the snowball at the top of the hill that has now been rolling for three years as I've grown into a stronger ally. I conquered that old irrational fear of the unknown with the simple realization that, homosexual or heterosexual, we're all just people, and to make a big deal of sexual orientation is to miss out on the rest of a person's identity. I could only come to this realization after living some time with a person who was both real and gay.

My reflections on my growth have left me with an awareness of one particular thing: American mass media culture has an inexcusable lack of representation of gay men and women. Had movies, television, or *Star Wars* novels during my youth incorporated realistic gay characters, not the ridiculous stereotypes, then I would not have been nearly lost to that fear of the unknown that we so easily ridicule until we remember its effects. In the gay and lesbian literature class that I recently completed, we often discussed how the lack of representation of gay identity has left gay men and women without a system of thought in which to understand themselves. However, this lack of representation harms heterosexuals as much as it does homosexuals; without positive figures in literature and media, heterosexuals have large obstacles in understanding and accepting our gay brothers and sisters.

Santi Thompson

More Than Just Sex:
The Folder in the Archive

DISCOVERING INFORMATION on the past experiences of gays and lesbians in South Carolina is hard to come by, so you might imagine how excited I was to find a lone folder, labeled "Homosexuality," at a local archive. The nerd in me was interested to see the folder and what fabulous information it contained. But my wonder and excitement turned to disappointment when the archivist approached me and apologized for what I was about to see. Instead of giving me a single folder on homosexuality, the archivist handed me a box labeled "Sex Issues." In the box, wedged between folders covering topics on rape and child abuse, was the folder on homosexuality. While I realized that the institution did not intend for this box to come across as offensive or inappropriate, I also understood the implications that a label like "Sex Issues" can have on our community and how it impacts the way that future generations remember our community's accomplishments and experiences.

For so long, mainstream America has relied on classic stereotypes to demonize the GLBTQ (gay, lesbian, bisexual, transgender, queer) community. Popular culture, politicians, and religious groups have characterized us as a group of sex-crazed men, child-abusing women, and a growing, militant minority determined to destroy every decent value and belief of mainstream America. The "Sex Issues" box reaffirmed these and other stereotypes. The only way to combat these stereotypes is to prove to mainstream America that the GLBTQ community is a diverse group of people who contribute positively to society in many ways. An archive, with materials on homosexuals, is an excellent place to find examples of positive accomplishments achieved by the community. This archive has only just begun to be created in South Carolina.

While I glanced through the contents of the folder labeled "Homosexuality," I realized that there were so many experiences from the GLBTQ community in South Carolina that were not being saved or recorded for posterity. I thought of countless people and places, just in Columbia, that should be represented in any folder on the topic. The folder should have contained materials that reflected our daily lives, which contradict the old stereotypes of the community. We are people who own businesses, pay taxes, raise children, and attend church. However, few of these everyday life experiences were represented. The long and outstanding work of organizations that strive to make life better for the GLBTQ community—like the South Carolina Gay and Lesbian Pride Movement and the South Carolina Equality Coalition—also were largely missing. When future generations look back at the struggle for marriage equality, will they have the resources to place South Carolina in the middle of that debate? When business leaders focus on workplace diversity, will they know about the work of the South Carolina Gay and Lesbian Business Guild? And as more and more cities include sexual orientation in their non-discrimination policies, following the lead of the city of Columbia, who will remember the 1992 Columbia task force and its foundational study of LGBT life in South Carolina?

The folder should have reflected gay culture and leisure. Columbia, Charleston, and other places in South Carolina have a long history of gay and lesbian bars that supported a largely hidden community. We know about places like the End Zone and the Fortress because people have been willing to share their stories and experiences. But there are other, more recent aspects of gay life that have been overlooked. Would we want the future to tell the story of gay life in Columbia without mentioning the performances of Samantha Hunter, Patti O'Furniture, and the other drag queens and kings at Cabaret, who not only entertain but have done essential fundraising for HIV charities and other community work? And how could anyone understand gay culture in Columbia without knowing about the gay-themed films screened at the Nickelodeon Theater and the discussions created by these films? The folder should have also acknowledged the diversity that exists within the community. African-Americans, Latinos, transgender individuals, and straight allies are all important parts to the larger story of GLBTQ life in South Carolina. Not including their voices and experiences would only silence their accomplishments and the larger story of our community.

Clearly, our community is so much more than a "sex issue." But it is up to us, and only us, to make sure that the future understands that. We are responsible for collecting materials that reflect the diversity and complexities of the community in South Carolina. We can all do our part by finding newsletters, photographs, and correspondence pertaining to gay life and culture and donating them to the South Caroliniana Library, an institution committed to ensuring that gays and lesbians are a part of South Carolina's history. In addition to collecting materials, I have a tape recorder and notebook ready to capture stories and memories of the GLBTQ community and look forward to working with anyone who is interested in preserving our experiences. Together, we can ensure that the history of our community is not silenced and that generations to come will know the rich, vibrant, diverse, and resourceful lives of South Carolina's gay and lesbian people.

Santi's commentary was part of a show announcing the creation of a gay and lesbian history archive at the South Caroliniana Library at the University of South Carolina. Rainbow Radio materials—along with Santi's oral histories and papers from the South Carolina Gay and Lesbian Pride Movement—are now part of that archive.

David R. Gillespie

My Religiousness, My Queerness

TWO OF THE INESCAPABLE REALITIES of my life have been my religious-ness and my queerness. And, as a result, much of my life has been char-acterized by a certain amount of either turmoil or denial—denial of my religious inclination in order to be true to my queer self, or denial of my queerness in order to express and practice those religious beliefs.

I grew up in the Presbyterian church, decided to pursue the ministry as a vocation during my last year of high school, and, in preparation for that, attended what is now known as Columbia International Univer-sity, an evangelical Christian college. I'm sure I wasn't the first queer at Columbia Bible College (as it was known back then), and I'm equally confident I wasn't the last. There were a couple of others there when I was. I know.

In graduate school—Reformed Theological Seminary—I simply turned off my queerness, or so I thought, by burying myself in my studies. But then, you can't really turn something like that off, can you? I was working for the ethics professor one year and helped him in the writing of a book on what he understood to be the biblical view of homosexuality. The process of doing that forced me to confront again who I was: a queer living in a straight—very straight—religious world.

Upon graduation from seminary, I was called to serve two small rural churches in the South Carolina Lowcountry. After developing a thing for the guy who played the piano, I left the ministry three years later, never to return, or so I thought. I suppose I decided at the time that the easiest way to avoid the turmoil and denial was simply to rid my life of anything that smacked of the church or religion. And, to be honest, in the early 1980s, forgetting was easy to do. There were plenty of distractions to be found back in Columbia, i.e., my first venture into queer club life.

After twenty-some odd years of turmoil and denial with an occasional sticking of my toe back in the waters of organized religion and quickly withdrawing it, and after returning to my hometown of Anderson, South Carolina, to care for my aging parents, I set myself on a course of reading and reflection to see if it were at all possible to reconcile my religiousness and my queerness. I am by no means the first or only one to have done so. Many have, and their names are familiar to many: John Boswell and Daniel Helminiak, and an outstanding nonqueer theologian, Jack Rogers. But I'm convinced that regardless of how many have traveled down that road, it is a journey we each individually must make.

I concluded that for me it was indeed possible to reconcile the two realities of my life without having to strip either one of its essential meaning or by trying simply to get biblical writers, especially the Apostle Paul, off the hook.

In my understanding, the Levitical laws forbidding male homosexual acts are clear and unavoidable; however, I think we have to understand the historical and cultural and religious contexts in which they were written—and for what purpose. I'm convinced they were written to make a clear distinction between the monotheistic Israelites and the polytheistic cultures among which they were trying to establish their own identity. They were also based on creation myths found in Genesis in which males are presented as those who penetrate and females as those who are penetrated. In other words, it was more about gender roles than simply sex. Besides, those laws occur in the surrounding context of a whole bunch of laws even the strictest of evangelical Christians today don't pay any attention to.

Paul was a Jew, a very conservative one at that, apparently. He accepted, not surprisingly, the Jewish view of sex and gender roles and, in his letter to the Roman Christians, broadened homo-sex prohibitions to include women. I have no doubt that's his view. Doesn't mean it has to be mine, however. After all, it's Christianity, not Paulianity.

Part of the impetus for my going back to study such matters was my renewed involvement in the Presbyterian church, specifically a small congregation called North Anderson Community Church, Presbyterian. What I discovered there was a palpable acceptance. See, I didn't want to be tolerated. Toleration seems to me to imply a "less than" status. I wanted full-blown acceptance, and I found it there. The jury is still out on whether folks like me will be able to serve in an ordained capacity in the national denomination, but there are signs of hope.

More importantly for me, however, I have discovered that as a queer Christian I can profess a deep and genuine love for God and commit myself to living by the principles spoken of and personified by Jesus of Nazareth—and not have to deny that aspect of myself we might call queer.

That's where I've come to in my own life and in my own understanding of what it means to be a queer Christian. I can be both. I don't have to defend or reinterpret Paul. I can say, simply put, we disagree. Now I can be faithful to my queerness and to the teachings of Jesus. No turmoil, no denial.

Candace Chellew-Hodge

Shipwrecking My faith

"YOU'LL SHIPWRECK YOUR FAITH!"

That's all my mother said to me when I announced that I had decided to go to seminary. As the wife of a Southern Baptist minister, she had reason to be concerned. Both she and my dad had attended a small Bible college in northeast Georgia—a place where you don't so much study the Bible as learn what Southern Baptists believe about the Bible. They attended a school that indoctrinated them into the faith and discouraged any sort of critical thinking. My mother was sure that if I started asking questions about my faith, I'd be doomed.

I wasn't so much worried about my faith running aground on the rocky shores of doubt as I was being an open lesbian on a seminary campus. I needn't have worried. I attended the Candler School of Theology at Emory University in Atlanta, a bastion of liberal thinkers—at least in my mother's mind. It wasn't a liberal theological playground by any stretch of the imagination, but, as I sat in orientation on my first day of school, I quickly realized that I would be right at home.

As we went around the room, several people, both men and women, openly declared their sexual orientation along with their faith background. When it was my turn to speak, I introduced myself and said, "I'm a lesbian, too!" By that time, any shock factor of such a revelation had long passed.

So, I settled into seminary, comforted and supported by my gay, lesbian, bisexual, and yes, even transgender, classmates. Until it happened—I shipwrecked my faith. In the midst of two semesters of Christian history, I arrived at the conclusion that only an idiot would buy into the Christian faith. Through the centuries of its history, followers of Christ fought one another relentlessly—squabbling over doctrinal and theological matters that would be laughable if the loser of the argument wasn't branded a heretic and killed in horrible ways by the winners—often called the "orthodox."

I decided that Christianity was like hamburger, filling and satisfying in the end, but you really don't want to see how it got made.

It upset me to no end that my mother was right. Here I was, washed up on the rocks, my faith full of holes. It took me another semester to realize that crashing and burning was the best thing that ever happened to my faith. Seminary, much like the military, is a place that is supposed to tear you down—to relieve you of your long-held beliefs and convictions—to help you question your faith and, in the process, build a stronger, more versatile faith that can avoid destruction on the rocky shores of doubt and despair. I realized that the faith I held going into seminary deserved to be shipwrecked—so I could build a better boat.

Even though Candler was quite gay friendly, it didn't mean the campus was free of controversy. During my time there, a small, but vocal, group continued Christianity's long history of theological squabbles. They circulated a flyer protesting the presence of gays and lesbians on campus and scolding the seminary for its liberal theology. School administrators offered to address the concerns of the group if any of them would identify themselves publicly and dialogue on the issue. The school declared the matter closed when none of the group would "come out," so to speak. The "orthodoxy" of Candler had won out, but these "heretics" escaped any official sanction.

It was then I realized that I was not the only one whose faith was being shipwrecked at Candler. The anonymous complainers seemed dangerously close to the craggy shore as well. I had never been directly challenged as a lesbian at seminary, but it was evident that my presence there was indeed a challenge to other students. They didn't feel comfortable coming out in the open and having a conversation about how GLBT Christians in their midst challenged their faith, but I hope that our presence sent a few of them up on the rocks and smashed their faith to pieces. It would be a fitting end to a faith that would exclude anyone from God's grace.

My mother always talked like shipwrecking one's faith is the worst thing that can happen, but my seminary experience taught me it's the best thing that can happen because it forces you to start fresh and build a better, more resilient faith that can withstand even the strongest storms of doubt. If my presence at Candler shipwrecked some more conservative faiths, then I'm glad for it. I can only hope those faiths have been rebuilt into more inclusive, loving, and grace-filled faiths.

Ed Madden

Words for Things

IT IS A STORY my mother used to tell with laughter, though I wonder if she does so anymore. Apparently, one Sunday over dinner, I asked what the dogs in the front yard were doing. I suspect that a lot of kids like me, who grew up in rural areas or with pets, were introduced to a discussion about the birds and the bees through just such an encounter with two animals. In our front yard, when we got home from church, there were two dogs doing what two dogs sometimes do: one was mounting the other one. My father tried to use the moment to carefully introduce a larger discussion about sex. I don't remember this incident at the dinner table—perhaps I've blocked it from my memory. But as my parents told it later, a look of absolute horror crossed my face, and I looked at my father and said, "You mean you do that to mom?"

Thus began my sex education.

I don't remember a lot about my sex education. Everyone lives with the scripts and misconceptions about sex they grew up with. But as a gay man growing up a in a very rural, very fundamentalist culture, I often wonder how I began to piece together who I was and what I was. Looking back now, I not only try to remember those bits and pieces of my education about sexuality—formal and informal, proper and improper—but I often wonder what messages were parts of those moments, and what effects those messages still have on me now, for better or worse.

From that traumatic moment with the dogs, I turned to books. Perhaps my memory is clearer on this because those books remained on my bedroom bookshelves well into my college years. Not long after the dog incident, my parents got me a book called *Wonderfully Made*, from a sex education series published in 1967 by a religious educational press. I recently found an old copy on EBay and bought it, just to remind myself about what I was taught so long ago.

Much of it is biologically specific yet vague, as one might expect from a book directed to fourth-graders: for example, "In an act of love the father puts the sperm into the mother's body," a statement at once biologically specific and totally evasive. The book is governed, of course, by heterosexual and reproductive imperatives, but I read back through it now, wondering where I found myself when I pulled that book from my shelves, even up into junior high.

Though the book insists boys will become interested in "masculine" things and girls in "feminine" things, it adds, "Everyone, though, has his own individual interests. Otherwise, life would become very dull. We hear of 4-H girls who raise champion cattle and of boys who win cooking awards. There is no reason for not following our own interests, even if they are slightly different from those of other members of our sex." *Indeed*, I think, remembering a little boy who preferred pressing dried flowers in his grandmother's house to learning how to fix things at his dad's farm shop down the road, the little boy who came home from church camp with projects of macramé and decoupage.

I also wonder, reading the book now, what I thought of the very end, where I was reassured, "Jesus, your Brother, knows all about the problems that growing up brings. He was once your age, and He knows how it feels." If Jesus knew how I felt, I don't know if I found that comforting or frightening, as I began to realize what I was truly feeling.

Of course, I wonder, too, how carefully I read the book when something like that could have meant something to me. Even a book like this has the dirty bits, and I'm sure that I mostly turned to the back to read that glossary over and over again—figuring out the words for things.

The only actual biology lesson I remember was a day in tenth-grade biology, where we got the basic mechanics I'd already learned from the elementary school sex-ed text, and then all the fundamentalist boys sat in the back of the room and argued over whether or not they were still virgins if they only had oral sex. (The consensus, years before Bill Clinton made the news with similar sophistries, was yes.)

My parents also gave me a novel, *Must the Young Die Too?*, a truly maudlin religious novel about a young man who descends the slippery slope of drinking and petting and ends up dead at the end. No surprise that the preacher who wrote it was the same preacher who baptized me at one of those summer gospel meetings, where my nascent sense of my sexual difference and my vivid fears of hell sent me down the aisle during the invitation song—inevitably, the song "Just as I am without one plea…"

There were other books, dangerous books. The marriage manual my parents didn't know I'd discovered at the top of their bedroom closet. Or the truly horrifying book, *The Homosexual Revolution* by David Noebel, which my mother got when I was in high school as she became more and more active in the religious right. I remember discovering that 1977 book in her closet of propaganda—and devouring it—only for it to disappear soon thereafter. Did she know I was reading it? Undoubtedly.

As the back cover says (on the 1984 reprint I found on EBay), the book is "an analysis of Gay Bars, Bathhouses, Bookstores, B&D, Churches, Diseases, Drag Queens, Epidemics, Greek love, Kiddie porn, Lesbians, Man-Boy Love, Marriages, Mass Murders, NAMBLA, Parades, Pederasty, Pornography, Preachers, Prostitution, S&M, Slave Auctions, Transvestites, and the non-Gay Politicians giving aid and comfort to the abomination." From that book I learned that "homosexuality is one of America's most serious moral and social problems," and that they are "a threat to the nation's children." And there at the back was another glossary, more words for things. I was discovering everything from bondage and discipline to Sappho, a Greek poetess from the sixth century B.C.—

and everything in between. Who knew that "Ophelia" meant gay hippie, or that a "Buckaruby" was a homosexual cowboy? David Noebel did, and he wanted his Christian readers to know, too.

Finding this book was a mixed blessing at best. What I might have learned about gay churches, gay politics, and gay marriage was undoubtedly outweighed by the extraordinary nastiness of the book's representation of gay people. The back cover's combination of churches and diseases, marriages and mass murders, preachers and prostitutes, suggests the double-bind of a book like this. As a closeted gay kid, I was learning who I was and learning simultaneously that my life would be one of murder, molestation, and disease. More words for things. Whatever I might have learned, I also internalized too many words for what the anti-gay right thought of boys like me: "deplorable," "deviant," "dangerous."

It would be years before I would discover good messages about sex and sexuality, years before I could return to the simple message of that first book: that "there is no reason for not following our own interests, even if they are slightly different from those of other members of our sex," that I am, indeed, wonderfully made.

Resisting

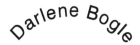

Leaving Exodus

WORDS ARE STRANGE. In the Bible, the Exodus refers to the coming out of the desert experience, and leaving the years of bondage to Pharaoh. It was coming into the promised land.

Exodus International has taken the name and the image to show how you can come out of homosexual bondage and orientation and enter the promised land of heterosexuality. They admit it's a long journey and there are casualties along the way. Support groups are established in almost every denomination and state, as well as in many foreign countries.

People of all ages, broken by the guilt of failure to overcome their homosexual orientation, seek out the support groups and follow rigid guidelines of retraining their behavior, supported by Bible reading and prayer. The arrival at the promised land is an illusion for most of the men and women on the journey because the premise is faulty. God will not change an orientation that He has given to His gay and lesbian children.

I directed one of those ex-gay support groups in Hayward, California, for almost ten years. We were known as Paraklete, the term for the Holy Spirit who comes alongside to give aid and comfort. I was a licensed minister with the Foursquare Church, and I had written several books and hundreds of articles on my "deliverance" from homosexuality. I was an instructor at several Exodus Conferences, and I appeared nationally on their behalf on television programs with Jerry Springer and Sally Jesse Raphael. I held down a full-time secular job in addition to all my "ministry" commitments and fully believed my lack of attraction to women was an indication that I was truly "ex-gay." I had been active in the gay community for over seventeen years, and now I was free of homosexual feelings and attractions. As an ex-gay leader, I was on the fast track, and I was a poster child for proof that the program works!

Imagine my surprise, shock, and horror when I realized I was wrong! I was the speaker at the Western conference of Foursquare women in the early '90s. The most beautiful woman I'd ever seen walked into the auditorium and sat in the front row. It was as if the final piece of a puzzle snapped into place and I knew she was God's gift to me. All the Exodus teaching and theology in my brain took a back seat to the intense attraction I experienced the entire hour of my workshop. It took a couple months to work out, but she felt the connection also, and we both knew that God was bringing us together.

We prayed and searched the Scriptures and challenged all the concepts I had been taught and was teaching at my ministry. God couldn't go against His own nature. He could not create someone with a homosexual orientation and then condemn that person for acting on those instincts. He couldn't call something sin that was His own creation! Exodus and I were not in agreement.

Exodus believes that homosexuality is a sin and that God needs to deliver you from that sin. I believe that Jesus saved me from every sin through His precious blood and that he didn't once specify homosexuality in all of His teachings to the church. Des and I shared our lives for twelve years until she lost her battle with breast cancer. She was totally amazed that all my "friends" in Exodus were not pounding at our door to try and woo me back to the fold. When I closed my support group and was asked to resign from the Foursquare Church, Des was certain those who were so into marking the change of hundreds across the country would not let one of their own go quietly. We waited; however, no such outreach ever happened. I longed to tell the story of freedom and my own exodus from the legalism of confusing being numb with being healed.

Last year, I read a book that changed my life and put the Exodus experience in perspective. It wasn't the Bible or a new pop psychology offering. It was a children's book, *Old Turtle and the Broken Truth*.

It tells the story of something that fell from heaven and was found by certain people. It was beautiful and amazing, and the people began to worship it. It had a message of truth, and the more they worshiped the truth, it became the only truth. It read, "You are loved." Soon there were monuments erected to protect the Truth, and no one seemed to notice that the object was broken, and no one wondered what else might be written on the rest of the object. Battles were waged over the Truth, and much opposition arose when anyone began to question the Truth. A little girl set off on a journey to find Old Turtle, who, in her aged wisdom, knew everything. The little girl found the Turtle, and eventually the broken other half of the Truth. She brought it back to the people and put it together with the side that read, "You are loved." Her half read, "And so are they!"

As children, we were told that sticks and stones will break our bones, but names will never hurt us. That was one of the first lies we believed, and it is a broken truth. We have spent our lives being wounded by rejection and cutting names that separate "us" from the saving grace of God. God sent Jesus to bring the healing balm of grace into our lives and draw us to Himself, not with a "blue light special" type of limited salvation of restrictions and guilt, but with a knowledge that nothing can ever separate us from the heart of God. That is the whole truth, and Exodus has spent over twenty-five years sharing only a broken truth. My mission for the rest of my life is to stand with my partner, Becky, and declare that God has created us and blessed our lives as Christians and as lesbians, and the whole truth is that He wants to do the same for you. Exodus's truth may be sincere, but it is a broken truth and, at that, it is sincerely wrong!

Christopher Renz

Walking into the Light

THERE ARE THOSE OUT THERE who believe that being gay is a choice and not something people are born with. I believe that people are born gay and do not have that choice. Many people have repressed their true feelings and desires for reasons of societal or religious acceptance and been led down the road to depression, regret, even suicide. I went down this road just two years ago. This is my story.

I was like every other kid. I went to a private elementary school and then a public middle and high school. I never really thought too much about homosexuals or homosexuality until late middle school and early high school. I always thought I was straight but knew in the back of my mind I was different somehow. I had never really understood anything about homosexuality. There were days where I woke up and just didn't feel like myself, as if there was something I was missing.

At the end of my senior year in 2001, I was accepted into The Citadel and attended that summer. As a freshmen, or "knob," I was kept quite busy with my schoolwork and other assorted chores I was assigned to do, so I couldn't really ever confront the issue of my sexuality. This all changed sophomore year. I was allowed much more time to sit and wonder what was wrong with me. I had the luxury of staying on campus much of the time because I didn't have a car, and many weekends were spent in the barracks. During this time is when the questioning began. *Am I gay? What if my parents know? What if the school finds out? Will I get kicked out? What will my friends think?* There were many days that I woke up and felt as I did in high school, that I wasn't myself and that something was missing.

I first considered suicide late in my sophomore year, after a weekend of extremely depressing thought and personal reflection. Gay and lesbian youth have some of the highest rates for depression and suicide. I was planning on taking every medicine I could find under my sink, lying down, and not ever waking up to the nightmare of my life. My attempt was inadvertently foiled when one of my classmates came in to talk to me about something of little importance. I decided to leave The Citadel after my sophomore year, so that I could fully confront my questions about my sexuality. When I went home, I did research about homosexuality but didn't find the best resources. Much of my search led me to sources like Jerry Falwell and godhatesfags.org, which pulled at my religious views. The religious condemnation of homosexuality drove me further down the road of depression, even while I was home.

In September of 2003, I met Steve Rodriguez. We met online and quickly became close, both having been through the depression, anxiety, and suicidal thoughts brought about by the condemnation of homosexuals. It was through Steve that I found my anchor to life. He continually encouraged me to accept who I am and to understand that we could get through the depression together.

There are those out there who do not know that they are not alone. I was one of them once. Are you? There are people out there who have been through the same troubling times as you. There is a light at the end of the tunnel. Accept who you are, not what others tell you is right. Look into your heart, and you will know I speak the truth.

Jonathan Jackson

Labels and the Gay Soldier

LET ME THROW MY LABELS AT YOU:

College student.

Christian.

Homosexual.

War veteran.

Does this work for you? Or do you have trouble fitting them all together at once? They're all true. They're all a part of who I am. When people start asking questions about me and find out that I was a gay soldier, there is always a moment of disbelief. A little cognitive hitch when those two puzzle pieces don't quite fit together. When they find out that I was a soldier for *five years* and that I served in Iraq, the pieces get even less compatible.

Labels can be good things. They become touchstones, categories, and shared languages used to explain our place in the world to one another. But they can come weighted with stereotypes and misunderstanding. And sometimes we have trouble fitting them all onto one person.

I imagine that people who never served in the military have preconceived ideas about tolerance for homosexuals in the service. The truth is, it probably varies depending on the branch of the military and the individual unit. Kind of like the rest of the American workplace.

I can't tell you about the military as a whole. I can't tell you about the Air Force or about medical units or about the Army bands.

I can tell you that I was in all-male combat units and that I was a leader in one of these units when we were called to serve in Iraq on less than a week's notice. I can tell you, with complete honesty, that I was good at my job and that I was respected by my peers. I can also tell you that many of the men who worked closest with me knew that I was gay, though very few ever discussed the issue with me.

And I was fine with that. You see, when I'm in the workplace, I try to be a professional. And for me that means not bringing my personal life with me to work. I'm not saying that I ever tried to hide my sexual orientation from my fellow soldiers. I just never discussed my private life at work.

I'm proud of the fact that I spent an entire year with my fellow soldiers in Iraq, working together, patrolling the hot, dusty streets of Baghdad, eating bland food together, sleeping on cots in the same room, feeling the same emotional and physical strain that comes with the workload and disorientation of a deployment. And I didn't try to make things easy on myself by pretending to be straight. I didn't feign interest in porno-graphic magazines or make up phantom attractions to famous women. I didn't concoct stories of sexual liaisons with women in my past. I was just myself—a soldier and a leader.

And the men around me came to respect me for the work I did and the way I treated them. After a time, many of them figured out my sexual orientation on their own. Living in such close quarters, sharing the kinds of bonds that only men who fight wars together have, trusting our lives to one another, there is an indefinable way in which the men around me just figured me out on their own.

It is an untenable state of affairs for our military to lose homosexual persons over petty, antiquated fears that are, ironically, already addressed by a comprehensive sexual harassment policy. The United States mili-tary loses an unknown number of valuable, talented individuals like myself every year because they choose to leave the military in order to live openly and with freedom.

I have a deep bond with and respect for all of the soldiers I served with in the Army. The fact that so many of these men knew I was gay and chose to respect me for my talent as a soldier rather than condemn me for my personal life speaks volumes about their integrity as human beings. I know that if this kind of acceptance exists in an all-male platoon of soldiers who are fighting a war together, then it can exist in any part of the military and in any situation. Military leaders often claim that the "Don't ask, don't tell" policy reflects the fear that same-sex soldiers in combat would be uncomfortable around an openly gay soldier. But I am a living, breathing contradiction of this fear. It's time to abolish "Don't ask, don't tell." Let the labels fit together.

Ed Madden

I Voted for Reagan

"I VOTED FOR REAGAN. TWICE."

That's what Joe Pitt says in Tony Kushner's Pulitzer-Prize-winning play *Angels in America*. Joe is standing in the men's room of a federal office building, talking to Louis Ironson. Joe is a closeted, married, Mormon attorney. Louis is a gay man who has been crying in the men's room because he just found out his partner has AIDS. When Louis complains about the callousness of the "Reaganite heartless macho lawyers" that work in the building, Joe says, "I voted for Reagan. Twice."

"Twice," replies Louis. "Well, oh boy. A gay Republican."

Instead of communists lurking in the washroom, it seems, we have a greater threat there: gay Republicans.

When I saw the play—both in New York and in Columbia—that line about "a gay Republican" got a big laugh. It depends on a certain stereotype: that being gay and being Republican are mutually exclusive identities. Or, that these two identities can only come together when someone is closeted, self-loathing, and self-destructive—like the only other gay Republican we see in the play, Roy Cohn.

I will admit that for a long time I thought the stereotype was true, since in my youth I was—like Joe Pitt—a closeted gay man who depended on religious and Republican ideologies to deny and repress my own sexual identity. As the president of the College Republicans at my little fundamentalist college in the early 1980s, I wrote editorial columns against gay rights. Unlike Joe Pitt, I only voted for Reagan once (I was only seventeen during his first election), but I could proudly claim to have volunteered for both Reagan campaigns.

I started being politically active at the local level when my dad ran for justice of the peace, a legislative position in county politics in my native state of Arkansas. In 1978, my freshman year of high school, I remember standing out in front of Remmel Church of Christ during the primary elections, passing out campaign cards for my dad. I was very careful to keep the right amount of distance between me and the front door of the polling place, a church social hall. The whole day, everyone was talking about Bill Clinton, the young attorney running for governor that year.

That same year, 1978, California citizens were voting on the Briggs Initiative, which would have prohibited gays and lesbians from teaching public school, and which would also allow for the firing of any teacher who could be accused of "promoting" homosexuality. That was the year the Log Cabin Republicans were founded, in part in response to the Briggs Initiative, and it was the year former California governor Ronald Reagan took a bold stand for gay rights, publicly denouncing the Briggs Initiative.

As gay Democratic activist and friend-of-Clinton David Mixner would later say, "[Reagan] turned opinion around and saved that election for us.... He just thought it was wrong and came out against it."

The next year, as Reagan began his presidential campaign, Jerry Falwell founded the Moral Majority. One of his fundraising letters that year asked, "Should school systems... be forced to hire known practicing and soliciting homosexual teachers?" Just as Kushner's washroom scene depends on inaccurate stereotypes about gay Republicans, rightwing rhetoric about gay teachers depends on inaccurate and reprehensible stereotypes about gay men, deploying fear and hatred of gay men to further a much broader political agenda.

Flash forward a quarter of a century—from 1978 to 2004. In a televised debate on October 3, 2004, Republican candidate for U.S. Senate Jim DeMint said that gays and lesbians (as well as single mothers) should not be allowed to teach in public schools. In advocating the firing of gay teachers, he only affirmed the South Carolina Republican Party's platform, which condemned the promotion of "unnatural or unhealthy sexual practices" in the classroom, and added, "nor do we believe that known practicing homosexuals should serve as teachers in public schools."

DeMint, who now represents South Carolina in the U.S. Senate, later apologized on NBC's *Meet the Press*—not for advocating the termination of gay teachers, but because the issue became, as he said, a "distraction."

With such attitudes entrenched in the state party platform in 2004, you would think South Carolina remains twenty-five years behind the rest of the nation, or that nothing about Republican politics here has changed.

But there is a difference, and that difference is the Log Cabin Republicans. In March of 2004, a chapter of the Log Cabin Republicans was formed under the leadership of Philip Bradley of Charleston. In May, Columbia-area Log Cabin Republicans hosted a booth at the South Carolina Pride Festival in Finlay Park—the first time there has ever been official Republican outreach at a South Carolina gay pride event.

In that, there is hope. As openly gay Democratic candidate for South Carolina House Charlie Smith said in early 2004, the growth of the Log Cabin Republicans in this state will only help gays and lesbians of both parties gain access in a state government that is largely Republican-controlled.

Gay people in this nation—and in this state—will never achieve equal status unless we work in both parties. Political work doesn't happen in a vacuum, and political progress doesn't happen in a closet. And the South Carolina Republican platform will only change when gay and lesbian Republicans in this state come out—as gays and lesbians *and* as Republicans.

When that happens, "gay Republican" will no longer be a punch line in a theatrical joke. Instead, gay Republicans will be among those making this state a better place for all of us.

Tony Price

AIDS Activism
in South Carolina

World AIDS Day 2005

THIS WEEK, throughout South Carolina and around the world, millions recognized World AIDS Day with a theme of "Stop AIDS: Keep the Promise." It is a call to action—a time for rededication of commitments and energies, a time to remember and renew AIDS activism. As I look back and reflect on the early years of AIDS activism in South Carolina in the 1980s, two things strike me as important to remember: the *why* and the *how*. *Why* was activism so important? And *how* did we carry it out?

The *why* is the why of many a social movement. Whether civil rights for racial minorities or equal rights for GLBT persons, there clearly existed inequities, mistreatments, and persons dying alone—kicked out of their homes and churches, and rejected or feared by socialand health-care agencies.

The *how* took on many forms: a small group of seven from Columbia, myself included, traveled to Washington, D.C., in 1983 to participate in a national march and candlelight event to enlighten the country about the

118

devastation of this new disease, AIDS. We were the only seven persons from our state; among the national participants were those folks who founded NAPWA, the National Association of People With AIDS, who spoke of living with AIDS, not being victims. Many of them are gone now, as are two of the other six folks who traveled with me from South Carolina.

AIDS activism from the African-American community was rare in the '80s, but two pioneers, DiAna DiAna and Dr. Bambi Gaddist, took it on, full force, with their efforts to put youth and women's issues in the forefront, using young peer educators in the AIDS Busters project and using beauty salons and barber shops in the Shear Devotion program to spread the truth and fight fears and prejudice, right there in the grass-roots of communities.

There were the smallest of acts, no less significant, like when Harriet Hancock visited a lonely Person With AIDS in his hospital room in Lancaster, being one of the sole persons to sit by his side and give him human touch. Shortly after, Harriet and I and others worked to form the state's first AIDS service organization, Palmetto AIDS Life Support Services (PALSS), because it was time for activism to take a shape and place in the community—to be an advocate for those too sick to speak for themselves at times.

There were the largest of visible acts, when ACT UP groups from outside of South Carolina worked with local community activists to stage a "die-in" on the grounds of the State House, chanting the now famous phrase "Silence equals death" for onlookers and the media to take back to local areas.

Recently, activism has come full circle with the South Carolina HIV/AIDS Council's mass media project to fight stigma and the national initiative known as the Campaign to End AIDS, locally spearheaded by a few dedicated people living with AIDS who want to be part of making a difference in this epidemic.

For everyone involved, from the early days of AIDS activism to these most recent efforts, it's not enough to let things be—to accept the inequities, the injustices, the stigma, the discrimination. It is essential to their being part of the human family to do something about these wrongs. It is a matter, literally, of life and death.

Twenty-five years into activism here and elsewhere, the message still rings loudly for us, and we must shout it out again and again and again, that truly "Silence equals death."

Who Let the Bears Out?

IT WASN'T UNTIL I LEFT FLORIDA in the mid-1980s to go to college in North Carolina that I really came out. I mean, I knew I was gay as early as middle school, but it was in college that I was given the opportunity to reinvent myself, far from the expectations of my family and high school friends. It was a slow process, but, during those four years, I went from telling a few friends, to anonymously authoring editorials, to co-chairing the campus gay and lesbian student organization, and finally to applying to the university president's office for appointment to his AIDS Task Force as an undergraduate representative.

Politically, I was very active. However, socially, I was inactive. Aside from support-groups and activist organizations, there wasn't much going on on campus for gay men and lesbians. I would sometimes venture with my straight friends to the gay club in downtown Durham, the Power Company, but I never really fit in. At six-foot-three, two hundred and twenty pounds, and bearded since I was a sophomore, it was hard for me to fit in with the preppy crowd—it didn't matter what color IZOD shirt or which Members Only jacket I wore, I couldn't pull it off. I was a bear before being a bear was cool.

About the same time I was reinventing myself in North Carolina, gay men a continent away in San Francisco were beginning to self-identify as bears. I'm not sure what series of events brought together the blue-collar aesthetic of the leather community, the disregard for size from the girth-and-mirth groups, and the fetishizing of facial and body hair—perhaps it was a backlash against the gym and diet crazes and the popular images of prepubescent *Blueboy* models; perhaps it was a reaction to the AIDS epidemic, which made people suspicious of the overly thin; or perhaps it grew out of a circle of friends who established a certain look to carve out their own niche in the Bay Area clone culture. Whatever the reason, the bear identity filled a need that went beyond California and beyond the United States, to eventually include most of the world. Bear clubs were quickly founded in other major cities and eventually filtered down into smaller and smaller cities. And, in 1993, one was founded in Charlotte. The area's first bear club, the Confederate Bears, was short-lived and quickly disbanded, and, in 1994, the Carolina Bear Lodge was formed.

This is where our two stories come together. After graduation, I wasn't ready for the next chapter of my life. I didn't want to return to Florida because the new *out* me was now a stranger to everyone I knew there, but I wasn't sure how to create a new life for myself. I continued to work on campus, but I was separated from the student life by the label "employee," though I was able to blur the line for a while. To meet other gay men, I got a second job at a local lesbian-owned dessert shop—where I was told at my first evaluation that I'd proven to them that I could work as hard as a woman—but I quickly learned that my honorary lesbian status didn't necessarily endear me to gay men. They were happy enough to have me serve them gelato, but, oddly, my apron seemed to detract from my potential as dating material.

But in 1994, while chatting online I learned about a chat-room called the Bear Cave. They didn't care that I wasn't boyish—in fact, they liked that I was six-foot-three and (now) two hundred and forty pounds and bearded. Where had these guys been? Certainly not in North Carolina. But then I learned about the Carolina Bear Lodge and, after meeting a few of them in Durham over burgers and fries, was invited to attend their open house in Charlotte during North Carolina Pride. I've been a member ever since.

Like those in other fraternal organizations, I've made lifetime friends. Not to overly romanticize it, but in some ways my lodge brothers are like an extended family. I've attended their union ceremonies, witnessed couples grow apart and separate, and even watched a few depart this world. And though some are just acquaintances and some have proven themselves to be fair-weather friends or simply troublemakers, there's still a bond we share.

That's not to say that the bear community hasn't had its own growing pains. Originally founded in opposition to the "clone" wars in San Francisco, it now fosters its own cloned images. The original rebellion against mainstream standards of beauty has given way to a new "bearish" standard of beauty that serves to alienate those who were once embraced by the initial openness. Beauty contests are a staple at all bear events, with the jock-strap category given much more attention than the contestants' actual service to the community they're competing to represent. While mostly just for fun, I believe these contests do have the effect of defining some people as more deserving of the "bear" label than others. Instead of self-identifying as bears, we're letting others write the definition.

Similarly, as the bear population has grown, so has the inevitable stratification. Everyone wants to be part of the A-crowd, or über-bears, as I call them. Some folks try to elevate themselves physically: where we used to scoff at ads in the gay rags for electrolytic hair removal and surgical pectoral implants, some bears strive to modify their bodies with drugs and extreme diets so they can qualify for the label "muscle bears." Others seeks contest titles and high office in clubs to guarantee their "über" status.

Finally, generational differences are putting some pressure on the bear community. While we're all products of our upbringing, gay men are also marked by their "out-bringing," that is, our psyches are time-coded to the era of our coming out. After twenty years of fast social change, the needs of the original bears and the newly-out bears (and everyone in between) are not always compatible, and, in some areas, multiple clubs have been formed along age lines. This separation saddens me in a movement promoting inclusiveness, but perhaps it's inevitable.

In conclusion, I'm not sure what the bear community will look like ten or twenty years from now, if it will even exist. To say that niche communities like the bears will disappear as the general gay community and society at large become more accepting is overly simplistic and naive. But to believe that the bear community won't change with the times is also naive. And as an "old school" bear, my challenge is to grow with the times and not allow my ever-increasing inner-curmudgeon to resent it.

Despite these issues, the bear community has been great to me and continues to be a great place to be: it helped me during a time when I felt socially isolated, and I've been able to help others out of their isolation. It is my hope that we, the bears, continue to welcome everyone with open arms and bear hugs.

Patricia Voelker

Lesbians of a Certain Age

WHEN I ATTENDED the first southern conference of OLOC, Old Lesbians Organizing for Change, I had to accept some numbers. Lesbians under sixty can't be members of OLOC and can only attend the conference as partners of lesbians over sixty. While I accept every senior discount offered me, this was the first time I've been part of an organization or activity where I wasn't the oldest. Nor the youngest.

It's not that I don't tell people my age. I do. But every time I hear myself say "I'm sixty-six," I wonder who is talking!

I remember clearly being in junior high in the 1950s and thinking that I'd be sixty in the year 2000—sixty obviously being an age beyond death to a teen. Now I wonder whatever seemed old about being sixty!

What comes to lesbians at age sixty besides membership in OLOC? Don't start listing ailments. Those can appear in our lives at any age. Being single? There were a number of single women at OLOC, but there were also couples who had been together for ten, twenty, thirty or more years. The ones who were single were open about their desire to be in a loving (and that means sexual) relationship.

125

Is one benefit of age less fear of being open? That's still a personal decision. The number of OLOC conference-goers who aren't out to family was far higher than I had anticipated, even though a number of them have been active and vocal for decades in feminist causes.

Is being looked up to as a conveyor of wisdom a benefit? Does that really happen? Next time a young gay man or lesbian asks you to share your hard-earned wisdom, please call me. The world in which today's young people come to know themselves is so different, it just might be that they have wisdom to share with us. At OLOC, I met women over sixty who were just coming out. The questions they asked could have been answered by gays and lesbians of any age.

Does being a lesbian of a certain age guarantee that I have grown up, matured, become centered—at peace, unshaken by hurt, never confused or indecisive, knowing exactly what I want and how to get it? I wish!

Age is a number. Each of us has a surplus of numbers to represent ourselves. Some would appear more the property of certain ages than others. Area codes and phone numbers, addresses including zip codes, social security numbers, cholesterol numbers, blood pressure numbers, weight, shoe size, dye numbers held secret by friendly beauticians, bowling averages, golf handicaps, the jersey number of your favorite football or basketball player . . . In fact we each have a numberless number of numbers that are our faces to the world. Age is just one of them.

At OLOC, my age was one number I found challenging. It's also easier to report than the other challenge, which is the number of times in my life when I've prejudged out of inexperience or ignorance or other remnants of societal enculturation. The problem here is that I don't know what that number is. I only know that I have to add one more to the mystery number because of OLOC.

OLOC not only restricts membership to sixty and above, they also insist on using the word "old"—not "older," not "elder," not "senior," not even "crone"—but "old." Some members even let their bodies reveal the aging process in a way that disconcerted me, in a way that brought up that prejudging that distresses me when it arises. I don't mean canes for those with titanium hips or weary knees. I don't mean double chins (which come with weight, not age) or even bald spots. I mean facial hair.

One woman, with a chin-full of gray hair, told of an encounter with a child and his parent. The child, noticing the lesbian's gray whiskers pointed them out to his mother. To the mother's embarrassment, I'm sure. The lesbian's remark to the child was, "This is how old women look."

Well, she's no older than I am, and the OLOC member who had both moustache and whiskers isn't either. So, it's one way old women look. But it threw me. Isn't all of this about stereotypes? Age brings certain images to mind and when they don't fit what we see, we get quotes like Gloria Steinem's "This is what sixty looks like." Old women have whiskers? Some.

Old lesbians are invisible. Not at OLOC. We may be old but we're still here—giving and receiving as we can, making noise, invoking change, claiming our place, supporting one another. An OLOC group in the Midlands would be a great addition to all the opportunities available for community. Or a Midlands group that includes gay males over sixty would be even more delightful. We have similar concerns, particularly health, housing, and financial concerns.

We have strength in numbers.

Wilhelmina Hein

A Journal of Transitions

AUSTRALIA, 1974: For years I felt that nothing was quite right. I had grown up in a very strict religious environment, and, as an immigrant child moving from Holland to Australia at the age of ten, I felt isolated through my younger years. Yet, something was not right with me. I discovered early on that I liked boys but also loved the feeling of girl's clothes and wearing them. I could not understand why my dad went ballistic when I spent the day sewing crepe paper dresses.

Now, in 1974, married, because my Christian counselor said that would fix those feelings, I discovered a book: *Conundrum* by Jan Morris. The heavens have burst open. I can name myself: I am a transsexual.

AUSTRALIA, LATE 1975: Great pain and great joy, separation from family. I am starting a journey after many fights with my doctor. Discovering a gender clinic within the public health system. Emotional raggedness: one day laughter and long-term vision, the next crying over the fact that I forgot sugar at the supermarket. What a crazy life on hormones.

~

AUSTRALIA, JULY 1978: Finally, after almost three years, a final assessment and I am approved for surgery. Divorced, holding a government job, having run and challenged the crazy requirements of the clinic—such as being divorced or having to move away to start in a new persona, which I chose not to do—I now wait for the call to be admitted to hospital.

AUSTRALIA, NOVEMBER 1978: Debacle. I was admitted, but by then the surgery was only performed in the state psychiatric hospital. I was the only one there who was sane. But administrative messes—the psychiatric coordinator forgot to book the plastic surgeon. With no support and a comment of, "Just go home. We will call you," I leave. Long running battles about surgery and when it can be done. What a mess.

After deep depression, my answer: Screw them. I decide that I'll go back to living as a gay man instead.

NEW ZEALAND, AUGUST 1984: Nothing's changed. I ran away only to encounter myself. I decide to go back to Australia as there is no surgery in New Zealand. In the meantime, three years on testosterone makes me butch and angry, still partly living as a man, now fearful of change, fearful of all the what ifs.

AUSTRALIA, NOVEMBER 1985: A poem, "Yet Again"
      Yet again, I fool myself
      Heavy eyebrows, dark beard, attempts at mustachio
      Yet the questions
      How would these earrings look?
      The feel of the material
      The cut of the cloth
      The price and whether I would need matching shoes
      Yet again, I'm fooling myself
      For through the cacophony of macho music
      I don't really feel at home in gayola city
      Is my tummy too big?
      Do I need a larger size of dress?

And when will this diet take effect?
Yet again, I'm fooling myself
For in the process of examination
I would still gladly find a scalpel
A knife, anything, and fashion according to longing
Anything in me that plays discordant notes.

NEW ZEALAND, NOVEMBER 1993: So much, so much. Another attempt in a private clinic in Australia screwed up when the original clinic doesn't send over their notes. Running away for a while, buying clothes of both genders. Finally time to stop running. There's a clinic here; it's private. They are willing to review my notes.

NEW ZEALAND, AUGUST 1994: Yes! Yes! Yes! I'm approved, *finally*. In the middle of everything on this cold, wintry New Zealand day, brilliant sunshine and the feeling that something is falling off me. I'm free, even if surgically I am not there yet.

CHRISTCHURCH, NEW ZEALAND, SUNDAY, NOVEMBER 26, 1995: Here I sit. A few hours more and my friend Joanne will take me to hospital. Imagine: surgery is finally here and two miles from where I now live, surrounded by friends and my congregation, surrounded by love. Tomorrow this time I shall be sex-changed. How has this God of life shaped my journey? Blessed be the Holy One's name.

CHARLESTON, SOUTH CAROLINA, NOVEMBER 2005: Ten years! Ten years since surgery. What a life and what a decade! Since then, I've completed undergraduate and graduate degrees, traveled the world with my pastoral work, even been able to change my gender legally as a Dutch citizen. All new diplomas, degrees, and transcripts from sympathetic colleges and universities. Life has been good—not without its troubles, but good. And not one day has there been any regret.

I am finally whole.

Melissa Moore

Strong Southern Women

I HAVE BEEN BLESSED with a Southern heritage. I have been cursed with a Southern heritage. Experience has taught me that a curse is just a blessing in disguise. A tool for change, if you use it well.

Born and raised in the Lowcountry of South Carolina, in Charleston, I am a child of economic and racial privilege. I am also a child of economic and gender inequality. Sounds like a paradox, I know. My parents divorced when I was two years old. My mother was one in a long line of pioneering Southern women, women who sacrificed honor and proper Southern ladyhood for liberation from the tyranny of their men.

I have many lenses through which I view the world. My father provided me with all the material luxuries a child could ever want. He is the picture of white-male economic privilege, and he is absolutely blind to it. Blind in the way that one cannot see one's own eyes; one can only see through them. He cannot see his privilege, he can only view the world through its shadowy lens. My rebellion was as much against him as it was against the part of him that exists in me. His blood courses through my veins, despite my mutiny. I am thankful for the lessons privilege has taught me. I have learned that privilege and oppression are connected—one cannot exist without the other.

My mother comes from a generation of strong women. I cannot begin to describe her until I tell you where she came from. My grandmother and her sister were the first women in our family to divorce their husbands. Divorce was unheard of in their day—and it is still a scarlet letter in some circles today. In the South marriage was usually expected of women. My foremothers carved a path for me. They removed themselves and their children from abusive situations, with little education and few financial resources. The women in the family rallied around them and helped raise their children. It truly takes a village.

I chose to live with my mother. Life as a poor, Southern, undereducated, single mother was unbearable for her at times, but she raised me well. She instilled in me a great tenacity and the fighting spirit which governs my life and my work today.

I hear people belittle the South and Southerners. They say that we are backwards, bigoted, and slow. I hear this talk from Southerners and non-Southerners alike. While our history is scarred with the legacy of slavery and institutionalized oppression, it is also a roadmap to liberation. There would have been no Civil Rights Movement without the South. Freedom fighters like Sojourner Truth, Coretta Scott King, and my grandma and mother have made this place beautiful. They have forever changed the landscape of the South and the world. They have carved out my internal landscape.

Today, we carry on the legacy of the Civil Rights Movement, the women's liberation movement, and the struggle for human rights. The South has produced the next generation of freedom fighters, and we proudly carry the torch of our foremothers and forefathers, brothers and sisters. All Southerners, be proud of your heritage, however beautiful or ugly it may be. Use the lessons of the past to guide the future, because as the South goes, so goes the nation.

I am shaped in the mold of those Southern heroes who fought and died for our human dignity. I am blessed with a Southern heritage. I am cursed with a Southern heritage. Experience has taught me that a curse is just a blessing in disguise. A tool for change. And I will use it with precision.

Alvin McEwen

Fighting the Lies
of the Anti-Gay Right

GAY MEN ACCOUNT for the largest number of child molestation cases.

Gay men have shorter life spans than heterosexual men.

Lesbians are inflicted with more diseases than heterosexual women because of their unhealthy lifestyles.

Gay men have more than five hundred sexual partners per year.

We have all heard them: the negative statistics, the lies and distortions that the anti-gay right uses to suggest that homosexuality is a disease and to support their claims that gays and lesbians should not have equal protection under the law. Many of us have laughed at the ridiculous rhetoric. But why do we laugh these claims off so easily?

Some of us laugh because we are trying to fight our demons. Inside of us, in dark places that we don't want to acknowledge, are remembrances of when we first heard the lies. For some of us, they were the first things we heard about being gay. They formed negative beachheads in our young impressionable minds. They made us feel victimized and helpless. They taught us to hate ourselves, to think of ourselves as sick. Was this the life we had to lead as gays and lesbians? Were we doomed to loneliness, disease, and an early death?

We laugh at their lies to keep them from reminding us of the frustration and sadness we felt when first coming out of the closet. We don't want to be reminded of the abject loneliness we felt. You know the loneliness I am talking about. The kind that makes you feel that even though you have many family and friends, you don't have one person you can come out to.

None of us want to be reminded of our past vulnerabilities, so we stifle the hurt we feel when we hear these lies. We pretend to be amused by the manic ramblings of so-called Bible thumpers. Meanwhile anti-gay and religious-right talking heads stand in front of legislative bodies, in front of church congregations and on television, spouting these claims virtually unchallenged, turning communities against us and giving those who despise us excuses for their hatred.

Case in point: the 2005 decision by our state legislators to push against marriage equality. In each of their mailboxes was a pamphlet distributed by anti-gay activists, "The Medical Consequences of What Homosexuals Do," which accused gays and lesbians of all sorts of evil actions, including eating feces.

In our zeal to keep our minds safe from persecution, we seem to think that if we ignore the lies of the religious right, they will go away. But an unanswered lie is a statement with as much power as spoken truth. And a community who wants to control how they are being portrayed must beat back negative images with as much fervor as it advocates positive ones.

How many of the legislators, pastors, people of faith, and, especially, people seeking to come out of the closet know that the anti-gay right repeatedly and systematically distorts news articles, legitimate studies, and books to make a false case against gay equality? How many know that anti-gay organizations rely on stereotypes and bad science to try to justify their religious and social prejudices, marketing hate under the guise of research?

Church leaders aren't aware of the fact that the anti-gay right repeatedly relies on discredited researcher Paul Cameron for their claims that gays molest children at a higher rate and that gays live shorter lives than heterosexuals—both false claims founded on stereotypes and unsupported by research. Church congregations don't know that the religious right distorted a 2001 Canadian study to claim that gays die earlier than heterosexuals. The original researchers of the study know this because they are the ones who complained about it. (For a fuller discussion of the criticisms of Cameron's research, see my book, *Holy Bullies and Headless Monsters: Exposing the Lies of the Anti-Gay Industry*, or Michael Kranish's article "Beliefs Drive Research Agenda of New Think Tanks: Study of Gay Adoption Disputed by Specialists," from *The Boston Globe*, July 31, 2005.)

I bet that very few state and national legislators are aware of how the anti-gay right takes statistics from the American Heart Association out of context in order to tell lies about lesbian health. And, finally, does anyone notice how many times the religious right changes the number of sex partners gay men allegedly have in order to suit the prejudices of whichever audiences they are speaking to?

Not too many people, if any, are aware of these facts. Unfortunately, this includes a lot of the gay community.

Despite all of their money and connections, the anti-gay religious right has one flaw: they don't operate on truth. They lie—and liars always leave a paper trail. It is our job to find this paper trail and expose it. It is our job not only to call out the lies but also to have the proof to back up our charges. We have to conquer those nagging feelings of helplessness. Every time an anti-gay talking head cites a study in order to portray our community in a negative light, don't laugh it away, and don't ignore it.

Get angry. Let the anger flow through you.

Then get educated. Look up the study. Nine times out of ten, the study has been distorted. Then inform everyone in your circle and your community. Write a letter to the editor. Start a blog. Get motivated to bring attention to the fact that there are lies out there about us, our communities, and our lives.

Let as many people as possible know that if these lies continue to go unanswered, they will negatively affect our right to protect ourselves, our children, our families, and our ability to achieve self determination.

Ed $Madden$

Just Desserts:
Family Recipes and Red Velvet Cake

August 2006, after Mike Huckabee's visit to South Carolina

PREHEAT YOUR OVEN TO 350 DEGREES.

If you're a busy guy like me, you recognize that as the first instruction on the back of the frozen pizza box, followed by the explicit directions to take the pizza out of the plastic wrapping before you put it in the oven.

But if you're a good Southern girl, who made her way through holidays and church potlucks, and who knows that the real stars of any church social are the desserts, or if you're just a good cook like my partner, then you recognize that preheated oven as the first step in the process of making something really good. Like brownies, or my Granny Lola's handed-down strawberry cake recipe, maybe even a red velvet cake.

Many folks know red velvet cake as that armadillo-shaped groom's cake in the 1989 movie *Steel Magnolias*. I remember it as my father's favorite birthday cake, and as the cake served at my wedding. None of that bland white stuff you usually get at weddings. No, we wanted something sweet and rich and memorable, that perversely Southern concoction of cocoa and vanilla and sugar and buttermilk and red food coloring—with two little groomsmen sitting on top.

The last time I had red velvet cake was in early August at a luncheon in Columbia hosted by two conservative organizations, the Palmetto Family Council and a small group called First Foundations. Special guest was Arkansas Governor Mike Huckabee. Relatively unexciting luncheon food—a sandwich with sprouts, some fruit—and pretty limited fare from the speakers' mouths as well—a few politicians advocating an amendment to the South Carolina constitution to deny gay and lesbian families and their children marriage, or any other form of legal recognition or protection.

But while those politicians blathered on about "classic marriage," I savored that sweet red velvet cake and memories of my wedding.

So preheat your oven to 350 degrees. Grease and flour a couple of nine-inch cake pans, and let's talk about cake.

In one bowl combine 2 ¼ cups of sifted flour and 1 teaspoon of salt. Set that aside. In another bowl—a glass bowl—combine 2 tablespoons of cocoa with 2 1-ounce bottles of red food coloring. While some recipes tell you to mix the cocoa with the other dry ingredients, mix it with the food coloring to guarantee that thick and consistent red. Don't skimp on the food coloring unless you want a pink velvet cake. And use a glass bowl, unless you want red-tinted Tupperware.

In your electric mixer, mix ½ cup Crisco or vegetable shortening with 1 ½ cups of sugar. (This stuff is good for you.) Add 2 large eggs, one at a time. While your mixer is going—say 4–5 minutes on a medium speed—let me tell you a story that Governor Huckabee told at the luncheon.

Huckabee told a story about the first time his son baked a cake. The family returned from a day at the mall and his son, who'd stayed home, surprised them by announcing he had made a cake—and he wanted his dad to have the first piece.

Oh, he was proud, Huckabee said. And he took that first bite, intending to praise his son, but the first thing out of his mouth wasn't those sweet words of praise. No, the first thing out of his mouth was the cake—which tasted awful.

The governor asked his son if he had followed a recipe. He said he did. He asked him if he was sure that he had followed it exactly.

Well, not exactly. He didn't know what a "dash" of salt was, so he figured a cup would do.

Put your mixer on low speed now and add the flour and salt mixture (just 1 teaspoon of salt in our recipe), along with 1 teaspoon of vanilla and 1 cup of buttermilk, then the cocoa and food coloring mix.

As I nibbled on that delicious red velvet cake from hotel catering, Huckabee smiled and explained. Yes, his son was sincere and filled with good intentions. Sure, he had worked very, very hard. But his son didn't know the definition. He didn't know the definition of a dash, so he made something that wasn't right and wasn't good.

It's the same way, Huckabee said, with marriage. You have to know the definition to get it right.

The analogy wasn't lost on anyone in the audience. All those folks who are working hard to make and protect their families—gay and lesbian couples and their kids, single parents, grandparents raising kids—no matter how sincere, no matter how well-intentioned, no matter how hard they work at it, they don't know the definition. So what they are making is just like that chocolate cake Huckabee spat out of his mouth.

Anti-gay activists like folksy stories like this. In the South Carolina House subcommittee hearings on the amendment last year, Oran Smith, director of the Palmetto Family Council, said, "If you take one gender out of marriage, you can't call it marriage. That's like taking chocolate out of brownies and still trying to call them brownies."

Why are these guys so hung up on desserts? Maybe it's because this kind of rhetoric makes the whole issue seem like a question of common sense. It's just a recipe, just a definition. But anyone who knows that South Carolina is fourth in the nation for same-sex couples raising kids knows that it's common sense to protect those families, not try to destroy them.

~

Make sure your batter is smooth, but don't overbeat it. Overbeaten batter—like overbeaten people—ends up tough.

Huckabee is a Baptist preacher, and he's sweet and folksy as he can be, even when he's telling you that you're like a cake made with salt. His bitter agenda of division and denial, couched in the sweet and folksy cadences of a family story about chocolate cake, reminds me that we need to add a little vinegar to our recipe. In a small bowl, combine 1 teaspoon white vinegar with 1 teaspoon baking soda, which will foam up. Fold this evenly into the batter.

Pour the batter into your prepared cake pans, bake at 350 degrees for 25 to 30 minutes. You will need to let the cakes cool on the rack for 10 minutes, too, before turning them out, and let them cool completely before frosting.

You can make a thick white frosting—old recipes call it an ermine frosting for the red velvet—with cream cheese, sugar, vanilla, and butter, maybe some crushed pecans. But it's really easier, sometimes, to just buy the cream cheese icing.

Sometimes you use store-bought icing. Sometimes you make delicious brownies without chocolate: they're called carob brownies. Sometimes you substitute vegetable oil for the shortening in these old-fashioned artery-clogging Southern recipes.

And sometimes you recognize that a family is made out of love and commitment, that not all families fit the rigid recipe that folks like Huckabee want to make into law.

Garnish your cake with raspberries and strawberries. Or with two little grooms on top. Sometimes, after all, presentation is everything.

Marriage Equality Week 2004

THURSDAY, FEBRUARY 12, 2004, Freedom to Marry Day, was cold, wet, and dreary. I spent the morning on the phone with my father, trying to explain that legal recognition for Don and me would not force him to accept something he disagreed with but would allow us to protect ourselves. It had nothing to do with religion and everything to do with treating people with equality under the law. (We still have this debate today.)

After the phone call, Don and I gathered with four couples from the South Carolina Gay and Lesbian Pride Movement (SCGLPM) and an array of supporters at the Richland County Judicial Center in downtown Columbia. We were nervous and scared, with no idea what to expect. As we waited at the front doors, we became aware that several police officers had begun to gather. We didn't know what this meant. We knew we were there to make a statement, not a scene.

During our work as board members with SCGLPM, we had learned about Freedom to Marry Day, February 12, recognized by gay and lesbian civil rights groups across the nation as a day to raise awareness about marriage equality and relationship recognition. We knew it was only a matter of time before the radical, national conservative push to discriminate against gay and lesbian couples would reach our state. As SCGLPM began talking about how we might recognize Freedom to Marry Day and put a South Carolina face on marriage equality, Don and I had already begun talking about a commitment ceremony of our own, a public recognition of our eight-year relationship.

SCGLPM planned a week of events, calling it Marriage Equality Week. The week would include a town hall meeting, various community events, and a public attempt by couples to register for marriage licenses—to show that there are gay and lesbian couples in South Carolina, and that we want to be treated as equals. Don and I had also decided to have our own ceremony at the end of the week, ending the public action with our private commitment ceremony.

Don's longtime friend and his wife planned to take part in the ceremony with us. When we met them for dinner to plan the ceremony, I was impressed by their questions. They were more than happy to do whatever they could, but only if they were certain that we were going to treat the commitment ceremony with all the seriousness of a heterosexual couple getting a legal marriage. I was amazed that it didn't matter to them that we were both men, only that we loved each other and that our commitment ceremony would be exactly that—a commitment.

On February 12, Don and I, hand in hand, started climbing the stairs to the second floor of the Richland County Courthouse, intending to apply for a marriage license. Though we were nervous, we realized that we were surrounded by our friends and supporters. However, my sense of ease left me when I reached the top and saw a line of police officers stretching down the hallway to the marriage license office. I told the nearest officer, "We're not here to cause any problems." He said, "I know, we're here to protect you." It was then I realized that I had been thinking it was us against them, when all along the "them" was already with us.

We were also surrounded by a crowd of reporters. As stories from San Francisco and Massachusetts began making national headlines, local TV and newspaper reporters became hungry for our stories, South Carolina stories.

The rest of the license process was somewhat of a blur. We filled out our forms and received the expected "Sorry, the law won't allow us to give you licenses." But the judge did add that if it were up to her, she would give us our licenses right then and there. This was exciting news. Many people were already on our side. We only had to get the right people to change the laws.

Friday morning. I had the day off from work to prepare for the commitment ceremony on Saturday. I called in to work and talked with my supervisor. He told me that the cat was out of the bag on what I was planning that weekend. It didn't surprise me because of the huge press coverage our registration attempt had received. But what he told me next did. "Some of your co-workers are very angry."

My heart stopped. My breath caught in my throat. I wasn't at all embarrassed of being gay or of my life partner, but my mind began to race. Who was angry at me? Would I still be able to go to work? Would I need to change cubicles or always walk with someone to my car? But then my boss finished. "A few of your co-workers are angry that you didn't invite them to your wedding." I was dumbfounded. I didn't know what to say. Once again I was thinking there was no support from the world around me, and once again I was surprised.

When I returned to work on Monday and finished showing off the ring, I was confronted by the one co-worker I was the most anxious about. The sweetest lady in my group was a grandmother in her mid-sixties. I just knew she would take issue with my being gay. I managed to avoid her most of the day until she cornered me at my desk. Then she pulled out a newspaper and proceeded to show me a picture of her grand-daughter, a lesbian, standing outside of a Chicago courthouse trying to apply for a marriage license. She went on to tell me how proud of her granddaughter she was and how terrible it was this action was needed, just to treat people fairly. And she congratulated me on the commitment ceremony.

If these events have taught me anything, it's that there is more love and common sense in the world than I sometimes think. People with the extreme views are the ones who speak out. The quiet ones will surprise you. Never assume someone will not support you if you don't have the courage to ask for it.

The Power of One

I WASN'T THAT NERVOUS, really. I had done door-to-door work before. But I could tell that a few folks in the room were. After all, we were planning to walk up to people's front doors and ask them for an opinion on gay relationships. One of our volunteers did professional car repossessions; she said she was ready for anything. At a state campaign strategy meeting last summer, several state activists argued against door-to-door campaigns, insisting that it wouldn't be safe, people would get bitten by dogs, someone might even get shot.

Having knocked on doors for an openly gay candidate in Charleston, including in some rural areas, I thought these fears were exaggerated. I believe strongly in the power of one person to make a difference and in the importance of this kind of direct, grassroots political work. Billboards and TV ads may be flashier, but I believe that nothing can be as effective as neighbors asking neighbors for their support and their vote.

So in November and December of 2005, volunteers from the South Carolina Gay and Lesbian Pride Movement met twice at the Harriet Hancock Community Center to do door-to-door canvassing. We were canvassing Melrose Heights, a small neighborhood in Columbia where the Hancock Center is located, and the neighborhood I live in. Most folks in the neighborhood probably know the Center, and we figured the neighborhood was pretty progressive since Kerry won here in 2004, and we figured it had a fairly gay-friendly population as well, given the number of university students and all those little Human Rights Campaign equal-sign bumper stickers.

In groups of two, we walked the streets, asking people to vote against the proposed constitutional amendment that would prohibit legal protections for gay and lesbian couples and their children, which would be on the ballot in November 2006. We told people we were volunteers from the community center down the street, making the politics local. And my partner and I told people that were their neighbors, just down the block on Fairview, making our appeal personal as well. Most folks in the neighborhood didn't know anything about the amendment, but most said that they would vote against the amendment.

All of the volunteers reported overwhelmingly positive experiences. Sure, a few frat boys yelled "faggot" through the closed door as one volunteer left their porch, and one guy tried to get into an argument about abortion (we didn't know where he was coming from). But most of the people we talked with were not only polite but also supportive. One elderly black man, wearing his Veterans of Foreign Wars cap, said that he served with gay men in the military and that discrimination was discrimination. One woman asked for extra informational flyers to pass along to her friends and family.

A few years ago, SCGLPM invited Georgia representative Karla Drenner to speak at the annual Pride celebration. Drenner is an out lesbian and mother of two who won a House seat in Georgia against the odds. She didn't have major funding, she didn't have TV ads, and she didn't even have the endorsement of Georgia Equality, the state gay group, which decided to endorse a gay-friendly Democrat rather than one of their own, since they didn't think she had the money or the clout to win.

But she did win. In Drenner's book, *The Power of One*, she tells of long days walking her district, meeting voters face to face, listening to their concerns, and asking for their votes. This is old-fashioned grassroots work, but it is still effective. And I believe it is the only way for us to run an effective campaign for the hearts, minds, and, ultimately, the votes of our neighbors.

When we meet voters at the State Fair booth or on their own front porches, we challenge old stereotypes about our community, we answer their concerns about the real issues, and we ask for their support. As we saw from our outreach at the State Fair in 2005 and 2006, surprising numbers of people will support us when we explain the issues to them—and when we ask them to support us.

We cannot afford a campaign based on television commercials and billboards and mass mailings. Nor do I think any of these things would ever be as effective as a neighbor asking a neighbor for their support and their vote.

But this kind of volunteer work is time and labor intensive. It requires a lot more people than the few folks who showed up at the Center to help us back in 2005, and it requires more courage, I think, than our community has shown before now. It means taking the risk of telling your neighbor that you are one of the people this amendment will hurt. It means having the courage to tell the married man next door, the divorced school teacher across the street, or the closeted gay man down the block, that their votes matter on this, and that they will be voting on folks like you.

We need a lot more folks like Representative Drenner in our community, and more folks like those few volunteers who showed up at the Center, or the fifty-six volunteers who helped at the South Carolina Equality Coalition booth at the State Fair in 2005, people who aren't afraid, who are not going to sit idly by during this fight and expect others to do the work, people who believe in the power of one voice.

I know that a lot of folks don't think we can win. The national organizations don't give us the funding or support they give other states, and some of our own folks don't think we can change things here in South Carolina. But I think about Karla Drenner's campaign. I believe we can change this state.

And I know that come election night in November—whether we win or lose—I want to have done everything thing I can to create change and empower our community. If we lose, I don't want to hear from any depressed friends I didn't see out in the trenches helping with the work. And if we win—even if we don't win the whole state but do win some neighborhoods—I hope there will be a lot of folks, more than the four people who showed up at the Center to do this work, or the fifty who showed up at the State Fair, to celebrate these well-earned victories. I hope that we will be able to say that we used this opportunity to its fullest, that we empowered our community in unprecedented ways, and that we did everything we could to make this state a better place for all of us.

The amendment passed in November of 2006. It did not pass in the neighborhood Bert and his friends canvassed.

Harriet Hancock

Walking Down the Street,
Holding My Son's Hand: Gay Pride 1990

for South Carolina Gay Pride 2006

FRIDAY, JUNE 22, 1990, was a hot, humid day, and the forecast for Saturday was more of the same, but with a possibility of thunderstorms. I'd been attending to last-minute details for the first ever Gay and Lesbian Pride March in Columbia, South Carolina, which was scheduled for noon the next day. My last errand that afternoon was to pick up the banner for Parents and Friends of Lesbians and Gays (PFLAG) before heading home, and I just barely made it before the store closed. When I got home, I made few last-minute telephone calls. One was to the Columbia Police Department—I wanted to find out the latest word on what we might expect in the way of opposition. There had been so many rumors about violence against the marchers, and I knew that the Ku Klux Klan planned to be there. The officer assured me that, no matter what, they were prepared, and they were there to protect us. But he cautioned me once again about the importance of keeping the marchers from breaking ranks and confronting the protesters. I knew that the street preachers would be there in force to taunt us with hurtful slurs, and it would be difficult to ignore them.

147

Later, my sister Diane called me. She must have known that I needed her reassurance that everything would be okay. She was so excited about the march, so upbeat and positive that it was downright contagious. I felt so much better.

I retrieved the PFLAG banner from the car and rolled it out on my living room floor. The white background with dark green letters would show up nicely, I thought. "Parents and Friends of Lesbians and Gays, Columbia Chapter." It was perfect. I had visions of all the brave parents, family members, and friends who would be proudly marching behind the banner in support of civil rights for their loved ones, and demanding an end to discrimination.

Yes, the big day was almost here. I thought of the energetic group of volunteers, the ones who had worked so hard and had endured those long Sunday-afternoon meetings in Marge Cooley's living room. I smiled as I thought of all the zany things we did to raise money for the march—the tricycle races, my first and only performance in a turn-about "camp" drag show. I was The Captain, dressed in white slacks, a blue blazer, a captain's hat, sunglasses, and a mustache that kept falling off. I was playing "Love Will Keep us Together" (on an air piano) while Patrick Barresi, as Tenille, danced and flitted all over the stage. People kept throwing dollar bills until the stage was nearly covered. Yes, we worked hard, but we had a lot of fun, too.

I thought of the friends that I'd made and how much I learned of their personal stories—of the discrimination they faced on a daily basis, the families that rejected them, and those who had not come out to their families for fear of rejection but were willing to come out and proclaim their rights and to rally others to do the same, no matter the price. Their time had come, and what an honor and a privilege to work with such a group.

I recall looking at the Pride T-shirt that I was going to wear the next day. It had the logo of a crumbling stone wall that symbolized the Stone Wall Riots in New York City in June of 1969. Stonewall was a defining moment in the history of the gay movement, and tomorrow was going to be a defining moment in the history of the movement in South Carolina—and I was going to be a part of that history!

The last phone call that I made that night was to my son Greg. I just needed to hear his voice before I turned in. After all, he was the main reason that I would be marching. I knew that he was a little nervous and a little scared. I think we all were. We wondered if it would rain, if there would be fifty or five hundred or maybe even a thousand people there. We hoped it would be a good turnout. We would be marching together, and we would be holding hands. We talked about the possibility of gunfire and decided that if we heard shots we would just fall down in the street and try to cover our heads. We were serious. I remember I somehow changed the subject and we had a few laughs about some funny incident. I wanted to end our conversation on high note.

I was fast asleep when the phone rang at about eleven p.m. The male voice on the other end was that of an older gay man, and he was very angry. He accused me of stirring up trouble for gay people. He said that I should just let sleeping dogs lie and "tend to your own business." He said, "There will be blood running down Main Street tomorrow and it will be on your hands." I was shocked. I wouldn't have been the least bit surprised if it had been a Bible thumper calling—but a gay man? I couldn't believe it. I was wide awake by this time and managed to tell him that it was time for gay people to let the world know that they would no longer be silent. That they would no longer tolerate the bigotry and injustice. That they would be marching for their rights, and for his too, no matter what the price. I didn't get much sleep after that.

Saturday was hot, humid, and thankfully overcast. Dark clouds were threatening overhead as I arrived at the Plaza Hotel on Assembly Street downtown, the gathering place for the march. I went into the make-up room, where we were offering to do face painting for those who wanted to march but were afraid of being recognized. We were so organized that we even had few professional make-up artists volunteer to help. No masks were allowed, but face painting, big floppy hats, and big sunglasses were okay.

I had been in touch with a middle-aged gay man from a politically prominent South Carolina family who wanted to march but didn't want to be identified. It was all about not disgracing his family. I had promised to meet him there and personally help him with a disguise. The room was crowded and bustling with activity, but I finally spotted him. I told him I was ready to get started, and he said that he had changed his mind. I thought he had changed his mind about marching—I'm sure he saw the disappointment in my face—but I told him that I understood if he felt like he couldn't march. He said "I'm marching, but without a disguise. I'm not going to hide anymore. I'm just going to be myself."

The time was 11:55, with five minutes to go before we stepped off onto the Main Street of our town. The sky was still overcast and threatening, but people just kept coming, gathering behind one of the many banners identifying each group—balloons with the Gay and Lesbian Pride Movement logo flying everywhere. People were hugging each other, leaflets with instructions on conduct were being passed out. Matt Tischler was there with his bull horn, parade monitors were taking their places, and Regi Solis was on his roller blades. There were gay couples and straight couples with their children, some pushing babies in strollers. There were dogs on leashes wearing the pride colors. My daughter Jennifer was there with her straight friends, and my two sisters and nieces and nephews and cousins were there. It was like a family reunion!

Finally, we heard the shrill of a police whistle, and we were off. I took my son's trembling hand in my trembling hand. We gave each other a squeeze, and we stepped onto Main Street. What a feeling of empowerment came over us—we were a part of history in the making! What an emotional time—we were so caught up in the moment that neither of us was aware that tears were streaming down our faces. I had held his hand when he was a carefree, suntanned little boy jumping the waves in the Florida surf. I had held his trembling hand in mine the night he came out to me. I had held his hand during troubled times, and I had held his hand during happy times.

But there was never a time quite as special as holding my son's hand, walking down Main Street, on June 23, 1990.

Contributors

SHAUN ALEXANDER was a public interest/poverty lawyer in north Texas until his relocation to South Carolina in the year 2000. He is a magna cum laude graduate of Southern Methodist University, a graduate of the Wake Forest University School of Law, and a certified secondary education teacher in North Carolina, where he teaches ancient and European history. He resides in Spartanburg, South Carolina. He is an avid book collector and hopes to publish more work in the next several years.

A native of Gaffney, South Carolina, JIM "jb" BLANTON was a co-founder of the South Carolina Gay and Lesbian Pride Movement, co-chair of the first South Carolina Pride (1990), and a volunteer producer for Rainbow Radio. Happily retired from SCETV, "jb" is a proud uncle and grandpa who has learned that coming out to relatives is a never-ending process that is occasionally infuriating, always exhausting, and often rewarding.

DARLENE BOGLE is a former director of an Exodus ministry. She was a speaker and instructor at conferences around the country and authored three books and dozens of articles while promoting the ex-gay ministry. She left the ministry over twelve years ago to build a life with her partner, Des, who died from breast cancer in 2005. She says that Des's last instructions to her were to go forth and share the whole truth of God's love for the gay community. Darlene appears in a newly released documentary, *God and Gays: Bridging the Gap.*

BRIAN BREITENSTEIN was a junior at the University of South Carolina when he wrote this essay. He says that what started as a creative writing assignment for his English class turned into an outlet for him to address a repeated issue from his childhood. Through this essay, Brian says, he was able to express his frustrations, ask his questions, and come to terms with his childhood personality. Currently, Brian lives in San Francisco and works as a retail manager for Gap Inc.

CHARLES CARSON, a native of Florida, moved to North Carolina to attend Duke University. Since his graduation in 1988, he has worked at Duke in several departments, currently at Duke University Press as managing editor of the linguistics journal *American Speech*. As an undergraduate, he served on Duke's AIDS Task Force, and, as an employee and alumnus, on Duke's LGBT Task Force. He co-founded the short-lived Duke Guild for LGBT employees, which was instrumental in establishing same-sex benefits for Duke employees. A member of the Carolina Bear Lodge since 1994, Charles has served on the board of directors, and received a Lifetime Membership Award in 2000 and the Billy Wolfe Leadership Award in 2001. He currently resides in Durham with his partner, Zac.

The REV. CANDACE CHELLEW-HODGE is a recovering Southern Baptist and founder/editor of *Whosoever: An Online Magazine for GLBT Christians* (whosoever.org). Her first book, *Bulletproof Faith: A Spiritual Survival Guide for Gay and Lesbian Christians*, published by Jossey-Bass, is now available at bulletproofbook.com. She currently serves as associate pastor at Garden of Grace United Church of Christ in Columbia, South Carolina. Candace is a media veteran with more than twenty years of experience in radio and television and is the co-host of Rainbow Radio.

Founder, co-host, and now executive producer of Rainbow Radio, BRUCE CONVERSE was born and raised around Chicago. With a forty-year working life in both the business and teaching worlds and stints as a part-time professional wrestler and a radio announcer, Bruce now teaches speech and communication at Midlands Technical College in Columbia. He has been active in the South Carolina gay and lesbian community since he moved to South Carolina with his partner in 2001. Bruce has also been the script writer for every Rainbow Rainbow episode since the show first went on the air.

BERNARD DEWLEY is an award-winning poet currently living in Miami, Florida. His work has been published in many journals, such as *White Crane*, *RFD*, and *Velvet Mafia*, as well as in the anthology *In Our Own Words, Vol 7*. His work was also included in the art shows The Art of Sin and Pinko Commies: The Art of War Censorship, Politics, and Freedom. Bernard won honorable mention in the 2006 Hub City Creative Writing Contest in poetry. He is currently at work on a novel.

Active in progressive politics and grassroots organizing in South Carolina for many years, BERT EASTER served on the board of the AIDS Walk in Columbia, where he met his partner of fifteen years, Ed Madden. He is also past president of the South Carolina Gay and Lesbian Pride Movement and a past vice chair of the South Carolina Progressive Network. In 2005 he organized the first door-to-door canvassing against the gay marriage amendment. He works at the University of South Carolina.

MELISSA GAINEY was an English and psychology major at the University of South Carolina when she appeared on Rainbow Radio. An aspiring writer, she is currently working on a book of short stories. She says her essay here is based on her difficult relationship with her mother and the conservative communities of South Congaree.

The REVEREND DAVID R. GILLESPIE is an author and speaker living in Greenville, South Carolina, who has published numerous short stories, essays, poems, and reviews. A former Presbyterian minister, he is now happy simply to attend a progressive Presbyterian congregation and speak here and there in a variety of faith communities. He loves living as a queer man in the "Christ-haunted landscape" of the American South.

CONNOR GILLIS is a young genderfabulous feminist, trans(national) activist, and radical writer who is deeply rooted in ideas of social justice and theory. This story is representative of the twenty years of his life that he spent living as a female-bodied lesbian in southern Georgia and the experiences that came with that. Now at twenty-two years old, Connor is socially transitioning and studying anthropology at the University of Georgia.

TOMMY GORDON's first exposure to political activism came when he was only four months old, appearing in the arms of his uncle alongside his mother and grandmother before a South Carolina House sub-committee considering a ban on gay and lesbian adoption. He was fourteen years old when he wrote the essay included here. He received the South Carolina Progressive Network's 2007 Thunder and Lightning Award for his activism and the 2009 South Carolina Pride "Straight But Not Narrow" Award. A talented musician and honor student, he was selected by the Duke Talent Identification Program. He is currently a student at Dutch Fork High School and plans to study law and politics in college.

HARRIET HANCOCK lives in Columbia, South Carolina, and is a member of Phi Beta Kappa and a magna cum laude graduate of the University of South Carolina. She is an attorney and mother of three children. In 1982, she started the Columbia, South Carolina, chapter of Parents Families and Friends of Lesbians and Gays (PFLAG). Since then, she has been a dedicated activist working to secure full civil and human rights for the gay, lesbian, bisexual, and transgender community. Columbia's gay and lesbian community center was renamed the Harriet Hancock Center for the Gay and Lesbian Community of South Carolina in her honor.

Born in the Netherlands, J. WILHELMINA HEIN migrated with her family to Australia at age ten, growing up in a Pentecostal denomination. In the late 1990s, Wilhelmina relocated to the United States to work full-time in pastoral ministry and theological education, both with the Metropolitan Community Church, and, from 2003, with Open Door Christian Church in Charleston. Throughout her early life, she says, she realized that "something was not quite right," and as an adult discovered that she was indeed transgendered. She underwent gender reassignment surgery in 1995 in New Zealand. Wilhelmina says that her gender identity has influenced much of her theological thinking. She left Christian ministry in 2006 and began the process of converting to Judaism, returning to live in the Netherlands in late 2006. She holds master's degrees in education and psychology and has a graduate diploma in religious education.

JONATHAN JACKSON spent five years on active duty in the United States Army and attained the rank of sergeant. As a section leader in a platoon of cavalry scouts, he led a team of soldiers in securing the violent streets of Baghdad, Iraq, for a year. After his service, Jonathan returned to Columbia, South Carolina, and completed a degree in English at the University of South Carolina. He enjoys talking to people about his military service and contradicting notions about what it means to be gay.

In 2008, LINDA KETNER, of Charleston, ran for U.S. Congress as an openly lesbian woman and lost to a four-term Republican incumbent by only four percent. She is the co-founder of Alliance for Full Acceptance and the South Carolina Equality Coalition. An advocate for the homeless and for affordable housing, Linda has also served on the executive committee of the YWCA and on the boards of the Riley Institute for Public Policy and the State Housing Corporation.

One of the founders of Rainbow Radio, ED MADDEN served as the show's executive producer for its first three years. An author, poet, and activist, he is an associate professor of English and director of the undergraduate program in Women's and Gender Studies at the University of South Carolina. Among the awards he has received for his activism are the South Carolina Progressive Network's Thunder and Lightning Award for outstanding community activism and the South Carolina Gay and Lesbian Pride Movement's inaugural Advocacy Award. In 2006, the Human Rights Campaign of the Carolinas awarded Madden the Legacy Award for a consistent and significant record of working to improve the lives and visibility of LGBT people in North and South Carolina.

ALVIN MCEWEN is the author of *Holy Bullies and Headless Monsters: Exposing the Lies of the Anti-Gay Industry* and the blogmaster of the website Holy Bullies and Headless Monsters. His columns have appeared on *Americablog, Pam's House Blend, PageOneQ*, and other online forums. He has also served as a board member of the South Carolina Gay and Lesbian Pride Movement and is a founder of Palmetto Umoja, an organization for gays and lesbians of color.

A native of Charleston, South Carolina, MELISSA MOORE was born with a passion for social justice. She attended the College of Charleston, where she earned her degree in sociology. She has worked toward building a more progressive and inclusive South through her work as a field director for the South Carolina Equality Coalition and as a volunteer for Southerners on New Ground, the South Carolina Progressive Network, and Women Advancing New Directions. She says she believes that progress is achieved when everyone has a seat at the table.

SHEILA MORRIS was born and raised in rural Grimes County, Texas, and is a first-year Baby Boomer. The two pieces included in this collection are excerpts from her book *Deep in the Heart: A Memoir of Love and Longing*, published by Red Letter Press and winner of a Golden Crown Literary Society Award for 2008. Red Letter Press published her second book, *Not Quite the Same*, in 2009. Her passion as an activist for LGBT rights has earned her numerous tributes, including the Human Rights Campaign Equality Award.

TONY PRICE was a co-founder of South Carolina's first AIDS service organization, Palmetto AIDS Life Support Services (PALSS), serving as its first board president. He began his GLBT activism in 1981 as the co-founder and first president of the state's first GLBT student group, at the University of South Carolina. In 1985, Tony was the first person hired in the state to work full-time in HIV/AIDS education. He was involved in the creation of the South Carolina HIV Network for the American Red Cross in 1989 and served as its director from 1992 to 2004. Tony is currently the program manager for the state's STD/HIV/Hepatitis Prevention Program.

CHRISTOPHER RENZ was a student at The Citadel in Charleston, majoring in English, when he appeared on Rainbow Radio. Born and raised in Lodi, California, he was an active volunteer for the South Carolina Equality Coalition, working many hours at the first gay and lesbian outreach booth at the South Carolina State Fair in 2005. He plans to pursue a career in teaching.

BECCI ROBBINS has served as communications director of the South Carolina Progressive Network since its creation in 1995. From 1990 to 2000, she was also the editor of *POINT*, a progressive news monthly that documented the best and the worst of South Carolina politics and culture—which she says was the hardest job she ever had, and the best. In 2002, she founded the Grimke Sisters, an online feminist community. Her other activist interests include animal welfare, environmental protection, and documenting grassroots organizing in South Carolina through photography and blogging. She is a graphic designer for Harbinger Publications and makes art in her home studio in Lexington.

Raised in Columbia, South Carolina, NICK SLAUGHTER received a BA in English and Russian languages and literatures from the University of South Carolina in 2008. While at USC, Nick worked as an ally in the SafeZone program. After having worked as a teacher for a year, he is now a graduate student in English at the University of Maryland. Nick is a hopeful younger writer and is finishing his first novel, *State of Nature*. He is the oldest child in his family, with five sisters and two recently-adopted brothers.

STACY W. SMALLWOOD, also known as Exodus, is a poet and health educator whose work has been featured in open mics, slams, workshops, and cultural arts events across the United States. He competed at the National Poetry Slams 2003-2006 as a member of the award-winning Columbia, South Carolina, Slam Team, which placed first at the 2006 Southern Fried Regional Poetry Slam. In 2004, he won the Shakori Hills Grassroots Festival Poetry Slam and was a finalist in the first annual Individual World Poetry Slam. His work has been published in *My South: A People, A Place, A World All Its Own*, and he donated recordings of his work to the Mahogany Pearls CD project, a benefit CD of poetry and music to raise money for Somali Bantu refugees relocated to Columbia. In 2005, Stacy was a poet in residence at Boone Hall Plantation as part of the South Carolina Heritage Corridor's African-American Poetry series.

While SANTI THOMPSON was completing his MA in public history and MLIS in library science at the University of South Carolina, he helped to establish the South Carolina gay and lesbian history archives at the South Caroliniana Library. Central to that archive is an oral history collection—a series of interviews Santi conducted in 2007 and 2008. Santi won the 2008 Student Project Award from the National Council on Public History.

TRIXIE TRASH is a video artist and drag performance entertainer living in Columbia.

Now a lesbian of a certain age, PATRICIA VOELKER says she received the gift of awareness of being lesbian at age thirty-nine. Raised in a culture in which homosexuality wasn't an option, she married, had a daughter, and divorced all within two years. She is now the grandmother of a grandson and two step-grandsons. A teacher in elementary, high school, adult basic education, and special education, she was also ordained in the Metropolitan Community Church and pastored MCC Columbia for eight years. Patricia recently joined the Unitarian Universalist Fellowship of Columbia, where she says both her sexuality and spirituality have found a home.

LAUREN WIGGINS recently graduated from the University of South Carolina with a degree in Women's and Gender Studies. She says, "I believe that it is never too early to educate children about the LGBT community, and personal accounts are crucial in this education." Children, she says, are not judgmental. If parents and teachers work together to promote awareness, "we will see greater acceptance in the coming generations."

BLANCHARD WILLIAMS lives with Don, his partner of almost fifteen years, in Columbia, South Carolina. He has helped mold the conversation and fight for LGBT equality in South Carolina since 2003 by serving on the board of the South Carolina Gay and Lesbian Pride Movement. He and his partner chaired the statewide Pride festival from 2003 until 2007, and Blanchard has served as Southeast Regional Director for InterPride, a coalition of Pride organizations from around the world.

ASHLEIGH WITT is a twenty-three-year-old resident of Columbia. An English major at the University of South Carolina, Ashleigh is currently managing a cosmetic line. She says she wrote "Prom 2002" to sort through painful memories stemming from the intolerance and fear her gay and lesbian friends felt in high school. Every few months, you can find her cheering for her old friend Cory, who unleashes his inner diva at a local cabaret.